Florence

WILMA ADELMUND-CONRADS

NEWMAN SPRINGS PUBLISHING
320 Broad Street
Red Bank, NJ 07701

First originally published by Newman Springs Publishing 2020

ISBN 978-1-63692-080-1 (Paperback)
ISBN 978-1-63692-081-8 (Digital)

Printed in the United States of America

Chapter 1

She was a thing of beauty with her long dark hair, slender-developed body, and lovely full red lips. When she smiled, her straight white teeth revealed a slight overbite. Her eyes were the color of the sea, nice and round and large, with long, full lashes sweeping over them like cascading waterfalls. Her brows were arched like beautiful rainbows draped over that sea of blue. She was full of the love of life, and she was bursting with energy. To her inner self, Hamlet, the small town she was living in, was stifling. It seemed ironic that the town had such an exciting, famous Shakespearian name because it was so dull. There was nothing to do here but become enmeshed in the dreams of the future. She wanted to see new places, experience new things, and meet exciting people. But she knew they were only fantasies in that incredible mind of hers. She seldom went to the movies, but Clark Gable was her idol. Oh, how she would love to actually see him in the flesh! Wouldn't that be great? Times were so bad that there was no money left to go to the movies. The country was still in the throes of the great depression. President Franklin Delano Roosevelt was doing everything he could to bring back a strong, healthy economy, and many people were working again. There was a new public works program, and she was hoping that when she graduated from high school, she would be able to get a good job. At this time in her life, however, there was still no money for frivolous things like movies. Every quarter was needed for the essentials of life. Trying to get the money together for the taxes on the farmplace was a major undertaking. They were due in another month.

The drudgery of going to school and doing the chores at home was unimportant in her scheme of things. "I want to see the world," she murmured to herself as she continued on her way home. The noise from the nearby two-lane Highway 30 caught her attention. "Oh, I wish I could drive one of those big trucks and go all the way across the whole United States like some of those truck drivers do. I know that Clark Gable lives in California somewhere," she lowered her voice as if it were a big secret. "I would just love to be able to actually see him in person. Wouldn't that be just wonderful?" She stretched the "o" in wonderful, which she shyly whispered to herself. She laughed a cute little chuckle and hugged herself as she wistfully dreamed that it was Clark Gable who was giving her that big hug. She jammed her hands deep into the pockets of her dress and felt the hankie all wadded up in there. She played with it as she sauntered in the direction of the house. She knew that she had better hurry home to help with getting dinner on the table. One of her jobs was to bring the water from the well for dinner preparation and clean up.

The year was 1935, and she was sixteen years old. Her mother, Ruby, and her dad, Josiah, had been in their early forties when Florence was conceived, and she was an only child.

The little farm on which they lived had been in her family for about ninety years and had no running water. She worried that her mother would have to carry the big pails of water for the evening meal when Ruby was not feeling the best. She had trouble with her back ever since Blackie, the stallion, threw her three years ago while she was trying to bring Mookie up to the barn. It had become apparent that Mookie was ready to deliver her calf. She was in pain, and in her rush to get to the barn where she would give birth, she bumped into Blackie just enough to knock Ruby clean off the horse's back onto the rocks, which were stacked by the eastern edge of the barn door. Old Doc Travis came and told Ruby to stay in bed a few days. He gave her a small box of little red pills on which he wrote, "Take one tablet every four hours for pain." She seemed to get somewhat better after several weeks, but she was hurting much of the time. When she was in a great deal of pain, she would take a pill—or sometimes two—and the medication relieved the pain, but it made her fingernails as black as coal the rest of the day and sometimes into the next. Ever since that time, it had been difficult for Ruby to lug much of anything.

As Florence neared the house, she saw Josiah by the stock tank and heard the familiar sound of the windmill squeaking as it pumped water into the massive tank. "It looks like Dad has already toted the water for tonight," she mused. She knew the routine: fill the kitchen buckets, then let the pump run until it filled the tank for the stock while the kitchen buckets were lugged to the house, then go back to the tank. When it was full, she unhooked the line, so the windmill ran free. This stopped the pump, which then kept the tank from overflowing.

"Hi, Dad. What's goin' on?" she yelled.

"I'll be up to the house in a jiffy. I'm almost done here," Josiah hollered back. "I came in early from the field, so I already brought up the water."

"Yeah, I figured that when I saw you there!" Florence yelled back. "See ya in the house." Lowering her voice, she said to herself, "I'll bet Ma is having back trouble again."

As she approached the front door, she could smell the bread baking and the sound of chicken frying in the pan. "Oh, yummy, that smells so good, Ma!" she shouted over the sound of the frying chicken and the clump de clump of the potato masher in her mother's agile hands as she deftly and carefully mashed the new potatoes. They had just been harvested three weeks before from the large potato patch less than a hundred yards from the house. You could see the tilled earth from the kitchen window. Josiah had already dug it by hand. As he dug each potato plant out of the earth, he would turn the soil over between each plant, loosening the soil. That way, it was ready to be replanted in the spring as soon as the frost was out of the ground. Florence greeted her mother with "Mom, how's your back today?"

"Okay, I guess. Did you have a good day at school, honey?" Mom asked. "You're home a little later than usual. I hope you didn't have to stay after school."

"Yeah, school was okay, and no, I didn't have to stay after school. I did have some questions for our history teacher though. We

5

are learning about the United States and the World War. Miss Soppe called it the war to end all wars. Did you know that President Wilson really did not want to get involved in that war?" Florence asked. "I wondered how America got involved when the president was not in favor of the war at all. She said that it had something to do with a ship or two carrying Americans being sunk. I can't really remember all of it. I guess the war was going on in Europe quite awhile before America joined in." Florence's face lit up as it suddenly came to her. "I remember! It was two ships, the Lusitania and the Sussex, I believe," Florence added quickly. "See, I do remember what I learn in school."

Ruby broke in with "I never did know why that war started or why our country was involved because I didn't go to school beyond country school's eighth grade. I just heard on the radio today that it doesn't look good in Europe right now, so I don't think that war will be the last one. Maybe there will never be a last war. When I think of all the lives lost in the last war and the potential for yet another one, it makes me shiver. Thank God I never had any boys."

Just then Josiah came into the house. "What's this about never having any boys? We can be so thankful that we were finally able to have Florence, our little beauty here. She is such a good girl and a good helper to us old folks. God has been good to us. We still have our farm where we can raise our own food, and we still have each other. You know lots of people these days don't know where their next meal is coming from. Most folks are still feeling the effects of the Great Depression. It seems to be getting better here, but in a lot of places, it is still rough goin'. Why, the Ryans down the road may still lose their farm. They've been working hard to get the money together to pay the mortgage, but Neal says he's not sure they are going to make it this time. We'll just hope things will work out for them." Josiah finished speaking as he finished washing up and sat down at the table.

The plates and silverware had been placed carefully on the kitchen table, along with the bowls of food. The chicken remained in the skillet to make sure that it was still hot when they were ready to eat after saying grace.

Ruby, trying to explain the conversation Josiah overheard, replied, "Like I said, I am glad that we didn't have any boys because another war seems to be brewing in Europe. There is trouble in Germany. I don't trust that Hitler guy at all. I wouldn't want to lose a child to a war. I pray every day that we can stay out of it. After all, the depression is bad enough for all of us. I can't conceive of another war. Most people can't even take care of themselves. How can we possibly pay for a war?"

They sat down to a good, wholesome, satisfying, and delicious meal. Ruby could bake the best bread! She had always been so proud of her wonderful pretty blue, copper-clad, coal and wood kitchen stove. It even had the warming compartments that were held up on the back toward the wall with a piece of black steel. They were situated on a shelf above the cooking surface. The warming compartments would keep the meal hot, as long as there was a fire in the firebox below the cooking surface. There were two compartments, one on each side. The entire meal was made using that stove, mostly taking advantage of their homegrown vegetables, fruits, and meat. The only things they needed to buy at the general store were things that they couldn't raise themselves, such as coffee, sugar, flour, yeast, yard goods, thread, needles, etc. Ruby was happy to live so close to downtown. It was an easy walk for someone who was healthy. At times, she sent Florence to town to buy some necessary items she needed at that particular moment. Most of the groceries were bought on Saturday afternoon after the house was cleaned. Josiah would start the 31 Chevy, and they would go downtown. Sometimes, they might even have a cup of tea in the hotel restaurant before they went to the general store.

Main Street downtown had a drugstore where Dr. Travis ordered his various medicines, pills, and poultices. He could be seen at the store sometimes when he wanted to make sure young Kenny Butler, who occasionally helped his dad in the drugstore, would fill his order to his specifications correctly. He really didn't trust the young man like he did the older Kenneth Butler. Dr. Travis's building was next door. Upon entering his very neat and immaculate office, there was a small waiting room in which there were several straight-backed chairs. Toward the back of the building, there was one little examining room and another small room to the right of that. In it sat a small desk and a sofa that could fold out into a bed. The sofa was used for patients who needed to stay because of a serious injury or illness where they could not return home after treatment. Dr. Travis lived on the upper floor of the building. That made it handy for him to care for any patient who needed to remain awhile so that he could be there at all times. Dr. Travis's wife was his only helper. Of course, she had no degree, but she was good at giving a lot of TLC. She would greet the patients and help as much as she could.

Naturally, she would leave from time to time to make sure that her supper was not burning on her stove upstairs. On Mondays, she also did her laundry, so most of the day, she would be upstairs. Each time she climbed down the back stairs to hang the laundry on the lines, she would check in at the office to see how things were going. The doctor usually was not all that busy because folks did not go to the doctor unless there was an accident, or someone was very ill. Many times, Dr. Travis went to his patients' homes. He could learn a great deal that way. Many times, he could tell by the conditions under which they lived how he could best treat them. He was a stickler on cleanliness. There were also diseases that were untreatable except to keep the patient comfortable. There were no antibiotics. He had no X-ray machine to tell if a bone was broken, although most of the time, it could be diagnosed by the feel or the look of the injury. If he was in doubt, he would cast the break anyway, just to be sure. He sat up many a night with a patient, trying to bring a fever down. Polio was something he feared most these days.

He remembered the flu epidemic after the big war that killed thousands of Americans. Whole families were wiped out with the dreaded strain of the disease. Many children still died of the flu, measles, diphtheria, pneumonia, and a host of other afflictions. There were few vaccines then. When a vaccine became available for smallpox, the children were lined up in schools and given the vaccine. The skin was scratched or sometimes cut on the surface, and the vaccine was applied to the wound. It usually left a rather large round scar on the outside of the upper arm. It was a successful program, and many lives were spared. Smallpox was a terrible disease that left the victim horribly scarred for life.

Polio was one of the worst. If the patient survived, they could count on becoming crippled. Some spent the rest of their lives in an iron lung in a hospital. The patient was placed in a large metal coffin-like machine that assisted the person in breathing. Dr. Travis hated to lose a patient, but most of all, he hated to lose the children. The one child he and his wife had when they were married a little over a year, he couldn't save. He was lucky that he didn't lose his wife also. It had been a difficult pregnancy, and things did not go well at delivery. He was heartbroken and never really got over it. It did, however, make him a more sympathetic doctor.

The Hamlet general store was on the corner of Main and Center Streets. The front of the store faced Main Street, and the side door opened onto Center Street. It was chosen by Mr. Mueller because the mill was just down Center Street to the left. There, grain was ground into flour. Further down Center Street was the blacksmith shop. There was a hotel in the downtown area with a diner on the street level. It was situated on the corner opposite the general store.

Hamlet was a unique little town. Everyone knew everybody and everybody's business. Naturally, there was always gossip. Most of the time, the gossip consisted of criticizing the people who frequented the beer hall down the street from the hotel.

Florence liked most of the people in Hamlet and could call them by name. She didn't care one way or the other about the people who went to the beer hall. As she was thinking about her town, she was fairly happy to live there. The people, on the whole, were pretty good people. No one locked their doors. Many had no locks on them at all. Josiah, as well as anyone who had the good luck to own a car, left the key in the ignition at all times. They didn't even think that anyone might steal anything. Florence seldom saw a stranger, and for the most part, she considered it her secure, nice town, even though she sometimes wanted to scream that there was no excitement and nothing to do but toil to eke out a living. Most evenings were pretty dull in her estimation.

The evening was generally spent cleaning up from supper, doing homework, and listening to the radio. While she listened to the radio, Ruby spent a great deal of time crocheting rugs, doing some embroidery, mending clothes, and doing hand sewing on the new garments she made for Florence so that she would look nice for school. Ruby even had a Singer sewing machine. When she moved the pedal back and forth with her feet, the machine sang to her. She usually used the machine during the day when it was easier to see what she was doing. In the evening, she didn't want to use it because that was the time the family wanted to listen to the radio. Pedaling the machine was just too noisy.

Ruby prided herself in making lovely dresses from flour and feed sacks. They were colorfully made and, if done well, could be beautiful, especially on someone as lovely as Florence. It was fortunate that the farmstead was close enough to the edge of town to have electricity. That was something many folks in this neck of the woods did not have. The radio was purchased from the Sears and Roebuck catalog last year, a year after the electricity was brought out to this end of town. Before that time, kerosene lamps were used for light. Two lamps in the kitchen did not produce as much light as the one single bulb in the middle of the ceiling. The Prescott family felt really proud when they had their electricity installed. This was Indiana in the 1930s. If you were fortunate enough to have your land and house paid for, you could eke out a meager existence.

The stock market had crashed in 1929, and Franklin Roosevelt was elected president of the United States in 1932. He took office in 1933, and by 1935, the depression was still being felt in most of the country. People who had invested everything they had in the stock market lost everything and were penniless. Some investors, after losing all they had, resorted to making suicidal jumps from tall office buildings in the big cities. This made it even more difficult for their families. Many people moved from their homes to try to find jobs elsewhere in the country. The farmers of the Great Plains had been experiencing droughts, which, along with many years of continuous cultivation, created dust storms, which, in turn, caused the soil to be carried in the air for miles. The dust was everywhere. It was so intense at times that it was difficult to even try to see to travel anywhere. The droughts not only made it impossible to raise a crop but losing the topsoil also made it difficult to raise any kind of decent crop because there were no nutrients left in the soil. This was a time of great distress, affecting almost everyone in the country.

In the cities, the people were trying everything they could to take care of their families. They stood in soup lines with cups in hand, hoping that there would still be food left when they reached the end of the line. Many families became homeless while others packed everything and went to warmer climates so they could at least survive. Some became migrant workers, following the crops as the fruit ripened, and the vegetables matured to the point when they could be brought in from the fields. They hoped to be hired to harvest those crops. New immigrants had an especially hard time because they had difficulty not only with the language but with the different customs also. They had the most difficulty being hired, but once they showed their desire and hardworking habits, they were some of the better workers. If someone showed a good work ethic, they could keep a job once they had one, if the company could stay in business. The problem was that people had no money and couldn't buy anything. Some tried to borrow money to live on.

Florence's family brought eggs to the general store regularly in exchange for other items that they needed. There was a great deal of bartering, where people traded a service or an item for something they needed, and no money was exchanged at all. It was especially common in the small communities and the farms around those communities.

Everywhere there was despair and disillusionment. There was so little joy or merriment in the land, yet there were those, like Florence, who dreamed of better times, better places, and having fun. "Someday," she vowed, "there will be a brighter day. I know there will be. There will be lights, dancing, and I will be able to have fun. Maybe even get myself a handsome boyfriend. I want to be free to really live my life to the fullest. After I have lived like I want to live, I want to have a nice family. I want at least two children so that no child of mine will ever have to be an only child."

As Florence, Ruby, and Josiah retired for the night, they were all praying for a better day—a time of peace, prosperity, and even, perhaps, a little fun. Things were going a little better lately.

Chapter 2

*F*ranklin Delano Roosevelt, a cousin of the flamboyant former president, Teddy Roosevelt, was elected president in 1932. At that time, one quarter of the workforce in America was unemployed. Banks were closing all across the country. By the time FDR took office in 1933, the economy had hit bottom. Everyone was looking to the new president for desperately needed leadership.

"I shall ask Congress for one remaining instrument to meet the crisis," he said in his inaugural address. "Broad executive power to wage a war against the emergency as great as the power that would be given to me if we were, in fact, invaded by a foreign foe." And then, with eight simple words, he won the nation's heart by saying, "We have nothing to fear but fear itself." It makes one wonder if he had some psychic power to have chosen those specific words at that particular time. Eight years later, those same eight words reverberated across the world and gave comfort to a land that was engaged in a war, the scope of which has never been seen again. It was a war that revealed horrors the magnitude of which mankind could never even imagine, let alone be totally involved in.

The congress granted FDR a mandate to lead, such as few presidents have ever been given. In just fourteen weeks, fifteen major bills were passed, shoring up the banking system, creating a huge public works program, and establishing financial safety nets for farmers and creditors. This was called the New Deal. This New Deal forced the country to take responsibility for its citizens. This ushered in unemployment relief and, later on, social security for millions of Americans.

With his visionary rescue plans, he invigorated the national spirit and changed the country's idea of what government should be about.[1] In other words, the government should take care of its people first. How can any country accomplish anything if the people are starving and destitute? What President Lincoln said in his Gettysburg Address, "Government by the people and for the people," President Roosevelt took seriously and acted upon.

Franklin Roosevelt was a man who did everything he could possibly do to help the United States come out of the worst depression to ever hit the country. Even though he was a victim of the aftereffects of polio, he was a relentless worker for the rights and welfare of the people of this country. He actually hid his condition from the American people because he was afraid that some of the people, especially the people of the opposite party, would think he couldn't fulfill his duties. Then he wouldn't be elected or reelected and, in turn, would be unable to help the country through the crisis and, eventually, World War II.

Florence was living in a desperate time in history. Little did she know that women had little, if any, rights. She just saw the nice little town where there was very little crime, nice little homes with nice, churchgoing families. Unfortunately, inside of some of those "nice" homes, things were taking place that no one discussed. It was not mentioned because nothing could be done about it anyway. It was a man's world in every sense of the word. Although women won the right to vote in 1920, long after former slaves, who were men, were given the right to vote, they still had no lives of their own. Even with their newly won right, many women did not vote because they were told that they didn't know enough about politics nor the process, to know for whom to vote. Others were informed by their husbands as to what their choice should be. Many women actually did vote the way their husbands did out of fear. There were those who took their voting very seriously and voted for the candidate that appealed to them the most. Thank goodness for secret ballots that didn't have to

---

[1]   Philip B. Kunhardt Jr. et al., *The American President* (Riverhead Books, 1999).

be approved by the husband. Many women felt threatened, so they knew better than to disobey.

In general, women were not allowed to go anywhere or do anything on their own. This was especially true when it came to those who had little or no money. The man of the house was in control of all money earned, and the wife had access to nothing. Women were simply another possession that a man owned, along with his house, land, livestock, dogs, and whatever else he had. Women had few, if any, rights. Men could do pretty much whatever they wanted with them. Once a woman was married, her entire life, soul, and body no longer belonged to her. Young girls had no idea that those lovely, romantic ideals of their teens would become only mirages for most of them. The future lives they envisioned for themselves would not be their reality.

Many decades later, former first lady Hillary Clinton would write about a young woman named Charlotte Woodward, "a nineteen-year-old glove maker who lived in nearby Waterloo, New York, who 150 years ago, knowing that if she married, working for low wages, her pay, her children, and even the clothes on her body would belong to her husband,"[2] not to mention her body itself. During Hillary's tenure as first lady, she pushed for legislation to point out the disparities for women's rights, compared to those for men, and attempted to close the disparities' gap. This is still a hot issue even today. Men doing the exact same job that women are doing are making more money. For a while, it was said that a man was "head of the household," which was the excuse that was given to allow them more pay. However, there are huge numbers of women today who are the head of their households because there is no man in the home. This was an economic way to keep women under the rule of the husbands. If there were children in the home, a woman by herself could not support the family.

---

[2] Hillary Clinton, *Living History* (Simon & Schuster, June 9, 2003). Memoir by Hillary Rodham Clinton, former first lady (1993–2001) and sixty-seventh secretary of state of the United States under President Barack Obama (2009–2013), written while she was a sitting senator from New York, p. 462, from a speech in Seneca Falls, New York.

Women were often burdened with many children and no money. They were taught that when the husband wanted to have sex, she was obliged to comply. It didn't matter that she was worn out from the daily drudgery of washing diapers, cleaning, cooking, and caring for the family. Many women were pregnant much of the time and not feeling well. The old saying "A woman's place is at home, pregnant and barefoot" was no joke—it was a reality. A woman was to obey her husband in everything. She was, in essence, his indentured slave.

That was a woman's life in those days when looked at realistically. Most women gave birth at home, and many died in childbirth. There were no birth control measures open to women at that time, especially for the poor. There was no birth control pill. It may have been wished for by many women but had not yet been developed. They actually knew little about how their own bodies even worked. There was no sex education. The only thing they really knew was that they were the baby factories. This was to be their destiny, and, of course, most women loved, nurtured, and cared for their children as they came along. However, they also knew that if they fulfilled their obligations as a wife, they were fearful every single month that they would become pregnant again. Every month they were afraid that there would be no menstrual period and rejoiced when their fears were dispelled. There was no planned parenthood where they could learn about their bodies and how they functioned. They had no way of escaping the vicious cycle.

There were good men, like Josiah, who truly loved his wife, Ruby, and did the best he could for the family. Florence thought everyone lived like that. She was an only child who was loved and wanted from the beginning. Her longing to have a more exciting life had nothing to do with who her parents were, where she lived or her life on the farm. It had to do with her inner self and her longing to see more of the world. The more she read about far-off places in geography and history classes, the more she longed to see more of those places. She would say to herself, "There has to be more to life than total drudgery each and every day. There just has to be. Is this what God really had in mind for everyone? I would really like to go to the places that are shown in the movies. Someday, maybe, I will.

Maybe I'll even become rich, so I can take care of Mom and Dad so they won't have to work so hard."

She was fortunate to be raised in such a good, loving, thoughtful family. Her ideas and Ruby's were considered when decisions were made. Florence was shielded from the realities of what life was actually like for many women living in that era. Women were treated as servants who were never to contradict their husbands or say anything contrary to what their husbands thought and said. This notion that women were inferior and, therefore, couldn't make any decisions on their own was also promoted and propagated by the many churches. The pastors would continually preach that women, in order to follow the Bible's teachings, were to obey their husbands. It was in the very vows that women repeated when they married. They had to promise to love, honor, and obey their husbands. Seldom did the pastors mention the part in the Bible about men loving their wives as Christ loved the church and gave his life for it.

Women also were brainwashed into thinking that every woman needed a man. In actuality, they did need to be supported by a man. The employment open to them could never support a family. The system was designed that way so women had to depend on the man to live. He had control over the finances. Therefore, he had control over her. They were taught that they needed to have children, or their destiny was not fulfilling. If the family was a farming family, many children were needed so they could help with the work on the farm. The more children, the more help would be available. Having as many as twelve or more children was not uncommon during this time. Grandparents wanted grandchildren, and it was also the duty of the wife to have those children so that there would be someone to help the extended family in old age. If a girl got to be as old as twenty-five without being married, she was considered to be an "old maid" and was spoken of derogatively. It was said that she was either not attractive enough to "get a man," or she was "a bitch," and no one would want her. Women's identities were hinged on being someone's wife. They couldn't really possess anything of their very own. They gave up their identities when they said, "I do." They no longer had their own last name, and for most women, it is still true today.

They had to give it up and take on the husband's surname as their own. They were now a Mrs. _____, followed by the man's first and last names. The United States of America was then, and still is, a patriarchal society.

One day, Florence came into the house after school very troubled. Ruby had some difficulty getting her to talk about what had happened. Finally, she blurted out, "Mom, when is it okay for a husband to kill his wife without being punished?"

"What are you talking about, honey? It is never okay for a man to kill his wife." Ruby returned the question with "What is this all about?"

"Charlene, one of the girls in my class, was talking after school," answered Florence. "And she said that she heard on the radio that a man in Texas caught his wife with another man, and he shot her. She said that her mom told her that it is an unwritten law that a man can do that under those circumstances. Is that true, Mom?"

Ruby hesitated for a little bit and said, "Well, I am not sure about that. Some people say that under those conditions, there is a great deal of jealousy and hatred and anger, but I think that they, at the very least, should have to stand trial. I hope that may be how the law reads here. Texas may have some different ideas, however. You know that each state, at this point in time, makes its own laws. This country has been set up this way because there is so much diversity as far as the people, customs, landscape, and level of wealth. Besides, this country is so big. Each state even has its own constitution."

"I know some of that already. We are learning about that in school," interjected Florence. "The point is that I am really concerned about those women in Texas. I wonder how many women there have actually been killed when they didn't even do anything wrong, Mom. My opinion is that no woman deserves to be killed like that unless she actually murdered someone on purpose. Even that would depend on the circumstances. Look at how Mr. Colpen beats up on Rachel. She always has some bruises somewhere or a black eye. She always says she fell down or something, but I know that is not true. I wonder how many states think like they do in Texas. It is scary."

Ruby quickly changed the subject because she didn't want to upset her little girl any more than she was already. "Let's get to serving supper. Your daddy will be in soon, and you have to fetch the water tonight. Now scoot."

Florence ran down to the pump, hooked up the windmill, and soon had two buckets of fresh water. She left the windmill running as she took the buckets to the kitchen. She helped set the table then ran back to loosen the line because the stock tank was full. She knew instinctively that Ruby was sparing her feelings about the incident in Texas.

When Florence went to sleep that night, it was a fitful sleep. She was thrown into a frightening situation, and she became the woman in Texas. She woke up with a start. "I don't think I ever want to go to Texas, much less live there," she said to herself as she drifted off again to a calmer and more pleasant dream.

Chapter 3

*I*n September of 1915, a daughter was born to two Dutch immigrants, Lena and Paul Viel. In the old country, Paul had been a sailor, and his job had been to sit in the tallest part of the ship, the crow's nest, to look out over the sea to sight land, other ships, etc. as a safety precaution. At that time, radar was not yet available. Lena had worked for farmers and also had gone across the border into Germany to work. Lena's family had immigrated to America and went to live in a small town in Iowa. There, people spoke the Platt (Low) German as well as English, so the language would not be a problem. Some of the extended families on Paul's side lived in Illinois, where many German and Dutch people lived. Immigrants had a tendency to go where there was already family and/or friends. In order to come into the country legally, you had to have a sponsor who had to be someone already living here. This was someone who knew you and could vouch for you. Many times, they would be the ones to provide the money for passage, would be responsible for taking care of them, get them settled, and usually had a job waiting for them here. The immigrant's arrival in the states was a time of rejoicing for those who awaited them. There was a huge influx of immigrants during this period of time.

In Europe, there was much turmoil, and living was tough. Most of the immigrants were people who were of a lower class and were destined to a life of total drudgery had they stayed in Europe. If you were born into the elite classes, life was a different story. The rich lived off the toil of the lower classes who could barely eke out a living, no matter what they did or how hard they worked. There was never a chance to better themselves or own property.

Here in America, Paul and Lena had a dream of owning their own land, and that dream could very definitely become a reality with a lot of hard work and frugality. Both sets of parents were already living in the states when Lena and Paul immigrated.

The little girl born in 1915 was greeted by her older brother, John. At this time, because of the constant moving to find work, they were living in Illinois, not far from the Iowa border, which was on the west side of the Mississippi River. The little girl was named Wilhelmina after the queen of Holland, whose name was also Wilhelmina. Her nickname became Minnie. She was a bright child. Paul was the love of Lena's life, and Minnie adored her dad. Lena bore two more sons, George and Ray, and two more daughters, Verna and Alice. As the oldest girl, Minnie tried to be a help to her mother, especially when the family moved to a different place. Paul had secured a job with the Illinois Central Railroad. The family moved to Waterloo, Iowa, as the railroad continued to expand.

John and Minnie were old enough to attend school when they arrived. They had always moved during the summer months so that a transfer to a new school would not be a huge change. There were several small towns where they were able to remain for a few years at a time. The small town where they spent considerable time was named Parkersburg. Lena's parents already lived there, so that was wonderful for Lena, especially since they had come several years before. She was delighted to be able to spend some time with her parents. She had help with the children, and they, in turn, came to know their grandparents. They also made friends there and naturally joined the church where Lena's parents attended. They could all worship together as a family. They became faithful members of the Reformed Church. This had been the state church of the area of the homeland from which they had immigrated. They found that this American church had the same rituals and beliefs that they were used to in Holland. They felt at home here. It was somewhat different, however. For one thing, they didn't need to pay taxes to a state church here in America. In Holland, even if you didn't have a membership in that particular community, everyone was required to pay taxes to the government for the state church. The Viels had belonged to the state church back in the old country. Here they didn't have to pay taxes to the state for the church's expenses. This was a welcome change. One could give as one's means allowed instead of having to come up with a set amount that was actually unaffordable for the family. Yes, they liked it in Parkersburg and were happy.

Paul was a person who was full of life and lots of fun. He had many friends wherever he went. He was handsome and had a beautiful smile with his shiny, straight white teeth that looked like a whitewashed picket fence. He had blond, curly hair that gave the illusion of a crown or halo when the sun was shining on it, especially when he had just washed it. He loved to look his best. When he walked by a mirror, he would push himself up straight and tall, stuff his hands in his pockets, bend back, and laugh. He would relish just looking at himself as he slicked back his unruly front lock. He knew that he was a very attractive man. He was tall and lanky, but he worked his frame gracefully as if it were a smooth, well-oiled, new-fangled machine. His eyes were the color of the seagrass that lined the dikes in Holland that he knew so well. He had a little devilish twinkle in his eyes that appeared as if they were polished jade, which stirred Lena's heart every time she gazed into those beautiful eyes. That was especially so when he looked at her in that one special way. Unfortunately, he liked to take dangerous chances, which, of course, set Lena off. She loved him with such a power that her heart ached just to rest in his arms each night. She feared for him because, somehow, she knew she wouldn't have him very long; therefore, she tried everything in her power to keep him safe and on the ground. She had premonitions of Paul being killed. She would repeatedly wake up in the middle of the night, calling his name after she'd had another nightmare of some horrible accident where Paul had been killed. She had hated it back in Holland when he was up on the tall masts of the ships that he sailed on. She secretly wanted him with her and on the ground where he would be safe. She was happy that he could no longer be on those ships, climbing the rope ladders leading to the crow's nest. The Midwest in the United States of America was the farthest from the ocean that one could get. Yet, from time to time, she still would picture him falling to his death.

While Paul was walking through Main Street on his way home from work one gorgeous summer evening, he happened to see Carl Wolfe. Paul decided right then and there to make an idea that had been cruising around in his agile brain for the last couple of years a reality. He actually made the bet. The little town of Parkersburg had the second tallest water tower in the state of Iowa. It had a small, steel ladder that went up to the catwalk around the belly of the tank and another ladder that went all the way to the little round ball on the very top. Only one man at a time could climb the ladder. He was definitely going to be that man. This town would be talking about this for years to come.

Paul came home that evening with an extra $50 in his hand. He handed it to Lena. Lena was horrified because she wasn't sure what Paul had done to earn that much money, but she was sure that it was something dangerous. She asked, "Paul, what in the world did you do to get this? Where did this come from? You don't look like you were in any kind of fight or anything. I know those Adelmund brothers are really tough. They are from Germany, and they are always in some kind of trouble. I just hope you didn't get on the bad side of them. I just heard again that they really know how to work hard, play hard, and are accomplished fighters. I hear that they are really good musicians too, and the one they call Paul is an excellent singer. He has a beautiful tenor voice. Come on now, where did you get all that money? You couldn't have won a fight, especially against them."

Paul was a little tongue-tied for a few minutes as he thought through the last hour of his life. He chuckled as he was congratulating himself inwardly at the gullibility of Carl Wolfe and the absolutely wonderfully successful little stunt that he pulled. He was smiling broadly and let Lena go ahead thinking and worrying. He wasn't going to tell her. She could have an acid tongue, and he really didn't want his feeling of success and the thing of beauty that he had done be ruined, at least on this day, this the day of his glorious feat and daring. He was reliving in his mind the last couple of hours after work today, this day. He giggled at what he had done.

He had made a bet with the most well-to-do person in town, Carl Wolfe. He boasted that he could stand on his head on top of the ball of the Parkersburg water tower. Paul had absolutely no fear of heights whatsoever, and he was really good at standing on his head anywhere. Lena was not with him this time. She didn't meet him at the station today, as she usually did.

Now was the time to make the bet. He knew that the family needed money very badly. He did not normally gamble, but he knew this was not really a gamble. He also did not want to upset Lena, so he just said, "Don't worry, everything is all right. Now we can pay our bill at the grocery store. We can also get caught up on the rent."

It wasn't long before the story was being told everywhere as to what he had really done. He had climbed the ladder of the tower deftly, stood on the ball first, and then promptly stood on his head. He just hung there as if he was being held up by an unknown force. Finally, Carl yelled at him to come down, "You've done everything that you said that you would do." Paul just hung there until the old man called, "Okay now, Paul, get your skinny ass down here before you get yourself killed. You have won the bet." Paul stayed there, his mind elsewhere until Carl finally yelled, "Damn it, Paul, I owe you fifty bucks, and I have it right here. Come on down and get it." It was only then that Paul very carefully let his legs bend and gently used his muscular body to begin the process of standing upright.

When that was accomplished, he yelled down at the crowd with both arms raised, "Yahoo, did you see? I did it! I did it!" Quite a crowd had gathered by the time the whole thing was over.

The house in which Lena and the family lived was a good five blocks away from the water tower. John, the oldest son, had heard some commotion but didn't go to investigate. He just figured the tower had been the subject of some visitors who would periodically stop to see the tall water tower. This was a common occurrence from time to time. It was beautiful to behold. The roof was a fire-engine red. The tank, the large pipe leading to the tank, and the ladders were silver, as was the ball on top. At midday, the tower would shine like a beautiful red and silver star.

Of course, being a small town, it wasn't long before everyone was talking about the daredevil Paul Viel. It was not long before Lena, too, heard about it, and she was livid. She was so scared of losing him, and here he was risking his life just to try to pay the bills. If he was killed, there would be no one to pay the bills. She knew this because she lived that horrible nightmare almost every night. The day she heard about him and his stunt, he was barely home when she started in on him trying to get him to change his ways. He needed to come down to earth and just be a regular husband and father. She wanted him to see his children grow to adulthood. Her fear of losing him made her overbearingly protective. He sometimes felt that he had no life of his own. He was a sailor, and he really didn't like the idea of staying in any one place too long. He was always looking to see something better over the next hill. It was just now that he finally realized that he might have lost his life doing such a stunt. It never really occurred to him before.

He finally said, "You know, Lena, you are right. I know that you are only trying to keep me safe. I really wasn't thinking. I just knew I could do it, and I could get us out of debt, so I never even dreamed that I might get hurt. When I was over the ocean in the crow's nest, I always figured I would fall into the sea, and I could swim back to the ship. When I was on the water tower, I just imagined it was the ocean, and I was back doing what I loved doing, if only for a little while. It was a rude awakening when Carl called for me to come down from my beautiful perch. I was having so much fun. I am sorry, but just then, I was not thinking about you or the children. I promise that I won't do anything like that again." In his mind, he thought, *Not for a while, at least.*

They clung to each other. Lena was crying quietly, and they were trying to reassure each other long into the night.

Chapter 4

When Minnie was five years old, about 1920, Paul was asked to move to a larger city to the east on Highway 20 called Waterloo. It had a crystal clear river running right through the center of the business district. Along the river, the electric company created electricity with the power of the water flowing over the dam. The Illinois Central Railroad had a roundhouse several blocks from the river, and it was the hub of the railroad. It was on the east side of the city. The railroad employed many workers. There were those who simply couldn't do that kind of work, and since there was a shortage of cheap help, many people from Mississippi came to the northern cities to find work. The Illinois Central put them all to work. This nice, small city now became a very diverse community. A new culture became a big part of this city. Paul, who had never even seen a "Colored person" before, was intrigued by them and wanted to learn more about them and their culture. He enjoyed working with them, and a number of them became his closest friends. They were working partners, as well as his friends. To him, it seemed as though they were kinsmen because they knew how to work.

There was a great deal of manual labor to do on the railroad. Paul, along with one of his fellow workers, often carried huge railroad ties that were being taken to the new track areas as well as to those areas needing replacement ties along the tracks. They were weighty and cumbersome, requiring that at least two men had to keep in step on the front end as well as the back end so as to keep it level and not jostle the tie so that it would be dropped. If one of the men were to drop the tie, the other partner's back would be wrenched so badly that sometimes men were unable to continue to work, or they would be laid off because they weren't able to continue the pace after injury. The railroad was a place where injuries were common. There were times when dynamiting needed to be done. Men lost limbs and eyes, and some were killed. It was dangerous work that, fortunately, Lena seemed to be unaware of. It was a job that Paul seemed to be able to keep, and it fed the family. He walked to work each morning and came home exhausted every night.

It was here that little Alice was born, about a year after arriving in Waterloo. She was a beautiful little girl with curly blond hair. She was such a happy child. She smiled a great deal, and Minnie enjoyed taking care of her. Minnie absolutely adored little Alice. She enjoyed her whole family. She had fun with her brothers and her other sister Verna also, but she delighted in helping take care of the littlest one. She would take Alice on walks sometimes around the neighborhood. She would pull her in the wagon, and all the while, Alice jabbered and laughed, especially when some of the neighborhood children would walk alongside the wagon and talk to her. What joyful times those were!

Minnie would go a different route as many times as possible to get to know the whole neighborhood. As she rounded the curve to walk by the house of the Sullivans, the boys were roughhousing on the front lawn. There were five boys in that house, along with a daughter. Aleta Sullivan came out and yelled, "George, you're the oldest. You should know better. You should be taking care of your little brothers, not fighting and teasing them. Now come in all of you and wash up for supper!"

"Wow," Minnie said to her friend Calista. "He has the same name as my brother. I wonder if they know the Sullivans. They look about the same ages."

When Minnie got home, she asked John, George, and Ray if they had ever heard of or met the Sullivan boys.

"Oh, yeah! They are really tough," replied little Ray.

"Yeah," answered George. "They are called the fighting Sullivans. No one ever wants to pick on any one of those guys, or the whole bunch will come at you with fists flying. No one gets on the bad side of the Sullivans. Their parents came right from Ireland. The Irish are great fighters, you know."

"Oh, I bet if I took on George Sullivan, I could beat him," John shot back. "We Dutch ain't no slouches either, you know. The only problem is I'd have to fight the whole family because I hear even the little girl holds her own against the boys."

Minnie countered with "I saw them in the yard today, and their mom really has them under control. They really respect their mom. She seems a little rough around the edges, but she knows how to handle her boys. She seemed to expect George to take care of the others and keep them out of trouble."

"That's no different than Ma expects of us," John answered. "I have to take care of Ray and George. And, Minnie, you, too, are expected to take care of Verna and Alice. That's just the way it is in a family."

Ray piped up with "Yeah, we all help."

"Come in for supper!" yelled Lena. "You have to get cleaned up before you sit down. Your dad will be here any minute. He will want to eat as soon as he gets home."

The children knew that she was just saying that because the food was ready, and she didn't want to wait much longer to serve it. She would never serve cold food if it was supposed to be hot. The meat dish, if there was meat, and the vegetables had to be hot. Lena was a great cook, and she served their meals on her only set of dishes. She liked to have the silverware placed properly beside the plate. Everything was served in bowls in the correct manner. Minnie had to take over watching the little ones while Lena cooked the food. There was a handmade tablecloth placed on the table before it was set. She might have come from a lower social class in Holland, but she was not about to act like it. She didn't act the part in Holland either. This prideful mannerism caused her to be taunted at school about not staying in her social class where she belonged. She was not about to act low class here, either. Everything in the house was always clean and neat as a pin. She was an excellent housekeeper and carried herself like a lady at all times, straight and tall. Even though she was only 4 feet 10 inches tall, she tried her best to look taller. She generally wore shoes that had a little heel of about an inch. They were black and polished. They had shoelaces that were tied in her unique way so that they resembled roses on the top of the arch. She had only one pair, so she took excellent care of them. She used petroleum jelly on a "shoe rag" to polish them. There was no money for real shoe polish. She also wrote beautifully, which she learned from her mother and grandmother, who were well educated.

She always wore a housedress with long stockings and an apron, which she removed before she sat down to eat. She had long dark hair, which she deftly twirled around and around so that it was nicely swirled into one large strand. Then she raised it up and plopped it all in the center of the top of her head in such a way that she only needed three large hairpins to hold it there. She looked lovely. Her hair was thick and lush. This style also added three inches to her height. Lena was always conscious of her small stature, especially walking next to her six-foot-two husband. Though somewhat large of girth, she didn't really worry about that because she was always so well groomed. She expected her children to be well groomed also. An excellent housewife, she prided herself on the fact that she was Mrs. Paul Viel. She enjoyed playing the part of housewife and mother and did a great job of it. She raised the children with strict rules. Paul, on the other hand, made everything fun, and the children did what he asked without resistance. Lena couldn't understand how he did it. Her method of discipline was to use intimidation, threats, or punishment. Paul's was to use incentives, praise, love, and making the chore fun. Lena spent so much time trying to please her husband, trying to take care of managing the house and worrying about where the money was going to come from, that she lost the joy of living.

When Paul came in the kitchen door, all the children from littlest to biggest ran to greet him.

"Daddy's home!" yelled the little ones.

"Come here, Alice. Give Daddy a hug," he said as he scooped her up into his arms.

"I have supper ready, Paul. Please come and sit down," Lena pleaded. "We are all ready to eat."

"Not before I hug my beautiful, hardworking wife," Paul answered as he sat Alice down in her high chair and took Lena into his arms and planted a kiss right on her lips. She was still blushing as they all sat down to have dinner together. Toward the end of the meal, Paul made an announcement, "Tomorrow, our whole crew is going to have a picture taken by the newspaper." Everyone was happy to hear that news because they might see their father in the paper.

The picture in the Courier showed a three-quarter shot of a great, black steam engine on which the entire crew was either standing or sitting. The engine stood in all its magnificence, covered with Paul and all his friends. Everyone felt extremely honored to have a part in this historic occasion, and it became a source of pride for the entire town. This was a major railroad company with a roundhouse and a very culturally and racially diverse group of men. This railroad was a very forward-thinking company, and they had a great deal of pride in their workers and what had been accomplished. Their tracks were always in excellent shape, which made the trains secure on the rails. There had been no derailments in several years, and the employees were proud to be associated with the Illinois Central Railroad.

Chapter 5

Everything was going relatively well for the Viel family until Alice was about five years old. The children were all in school except Alice. Kindergarten had not yet become a reality across the country.

In the early afternoon, a knock sounded at the door of the small home on Cottage Street. When Lena went to answer the door, three men from the railroad were standing on the doorstep. The tall man, Mr. Stephens, introduced himself and said, "I have some bad news, Mrs. Viel. Your husband had an accident today. It is nothing serious, but he is at the hospital on Logan Avenue. He and Charlie Reed were carrying a big railroad tie, and Charlie stumbled and dropped the tie, wrenching Paul's back as he was carrying the other end. The doctor wants to keep him in the hospital awhile."

Lena was beside herself. She kept asking, "Are you sure he is okay?" and, "Please take me to him." Her only thoughts were of her handsome, strong, wonderful husband whom she worshipped. "I can't lose him. I just can't. What will happen to us if anything happens to him?"

When she arrived at the hospital, dragging Alice with her, she saw her husband, his face pale and contorted, visibly revealing the suffering he was experiencing. Lena somehow didn't feel right about the situation. Paul assured her, between gasps of pain, that the hospital was doing everything possible to ease his suffering, and she shouldn't worry. "How can I not worry?" she queried. "I am so afraid of losing you, and Alice is not well either. She seems to have such a terrible cold. I don't know what to do." She began to cry, and Paul, in pain, could not comfort her. Alice was whimpering and coughing. The nurses did their best to help, but Lena was not to be comforted. She was finally taken to a waiting room so that her husband could get some much-needed rest. Mr. Stephens went with her and, after much convincing, helped her get home.

The other children were home from school when she arrived home, all of whom were hungry. She set about cooking up some kale "mitt'n Stück Speck" and barley. This is what the Dutch called a piece of slab bacon. It was not much, but it kept the children fed. She always raised some kale no matter where she lived. It was an exhausting time for the Viel family. Lena tried her best to see Paul as much as humanly possible. Her money was running low, and she fretted about each penny she had to spend.

A few weeks later, it was decided that since the railroad had a special interest in a hospital in Chicago, Paul should be taken by train to that hospital, where, in the opinions of the railroad officials, he would receive better care. He was told that the doctors on staff there had skills that were advanced beyond what a small city could provide. Paul should have been getting better after a week's bed rest, but the pain would not subside. His entire back seemed to be aflame, and he had difficulty moving his legs.

He decided that he would have to endure the trip. He was not getting any better, and he was afraid of the expense. There was no health insurance in those days. And no one could afford it if there had been. However, the hospital in Chicago was under the control of the railroad, and the management might help him with the expenses. After all, he was injured while he was working for the company. There were no unions, and nothing was a certainty, but he hoped and prayed for the best. It was up to the benevolence of those over him in the chain of command that determined how the situation would play out.

He looked out the window as the train slowly left the station. On the platform, he saw his beloved wife, Lena, waving to him and blowing kisses. Little Alice was with her blowing kisses to her daddy, her chubby little hands waving and throwing the kisses with all her might to make sure that her daddy could catch them.

Paul would never lay eyes on his active, pretty little blond, curly-headed five-year-old baby again—at least not while she was alive. Two weeks after Paul was taken to Chicago, Alice began running a high fever. She had a hacking cough, and all the nights Lena spent cooling Alice's brow did no good. Lena finally took her to the doctor, who recommended that Alice be taken to the hospital immediately.

There it was determined that Alice had double pneumonia. Antibiotics were still a thing of the future, and after six days in the hospital, the precious little girl passed away. Lena was beside herself. She had no money, and although her husband had always worked, they lived from paycheck to paycheck. She didn't know what to do. How could she pay for a funeral? How could she get through this alone? What would she do without her little Alice? She was the joy of her life. What would Paul say? Had she really done everything possible to save her child, or had she worried so much about the love of her life that she didn't realize that Alice was so sick? She couldn't get that thought out of her mind.

Lena blamed herself. She had nowhere to turn. She was overcome with grief and self-loathing. She simply went through the motions of caring for her five other children to the best of her ability.

She finally thought of her church in Parkersburg. Would anyone there be able to help her? The hospital called the Parkersburg church, and the pastor remembered the family. In those days, few people had cars, and even though Parkersburg was not far away, the family had not become involved in any church at this point in time. Paul's railroad boss arranged for Paul to be taken from Chicago to the funeral and again returned to the hospital. The pastor at their church had taken care of everything. At least that is what Lena thought. They even provided lunch after going to the cemetery. Everyone seemed so thoughtful and kind. Her thoughts, at the moment, were that she had an opportunity to see Paul, and he would be there to help her through the misery. This was the worst thing she had ever gone through. Paul didn't seem much better, and that also worried her. Right now, she was basking in the joy of seeing her beloved husband and thankful that he could be there with her for the funeral of her beautiful little girl. She would never see Alice as a teenager or an adult. She would not see Alice as she went on her first date. She would never again see her beautiful smile. This was the last time she would ever see her lovely little girl with the blond curls. She had difficulty standing up. She wanted to lean on Paul, but he was still in pain and could barely stand himself much less hold her erect. Then the realization hit her. Paul wouldn't be coming home with her. She lost control at that point and seemed to just fade into oblivion.

When she awoke, there were many people staring down at her, and for a moment, she wondered where she was. Her five children were there with her, and then she saw Paul, who was trying his best to bring her back to reality. John was being the brave little man. He was always the staunch one who kept his emotions in check. George was very serious even though his heart was breaking, and Ray wasn't really sure what was happening. "Mom, get up," he kept saying, asking others around, "She isn't dead too, is she? Alice won't get up, and they say she's dead. Dad, what is dead?" Little Verna seemed in a daze. She just stood looking at her mother.

Wilhelmina came to the rescue and took Ray in her arms, along with Verna by the hand, and took them outside for a little explanation. It seemed that Minnie always knew what to say and do. She had taken care of the children almost exclusively since Daddy had gone away, and Alice was hospitalized. Minnie was the confidant for all the children most of her life. She had an uncanny knack for reading people. She understood people's motivations for the things they did. Even at age eight, she was amazingly accurate at predicting how her brothers and sister would react at any given time. It was that gift that she brought to this situation. Her heart was breaking, but she was strong. Somehow, she instinctively knew how to handle things.

When the family got on the train to go back home to Waterloo and the little house on Cottage Street, Paul said his goodbyes and remained on the train.

He was headed back to Chicago—not home with Lena and the children, but back to that dirty city, and he hated it. He was always hoping that one of the many medicines that they were using on him would stem the pain and allow him to be normal again.

Chapter 6

*T*he news from Chicago was never very encouraging. Paul had been gone three months when Mr. Stephens came to the door again. He began to speak, "Hello, Mrs. Viel. I'd like to tell you that Paul is going to be released from the hospital in Chicago day after tomorrow, and I have arranged for you to go by train to meet him. He will need continued care at home."

"Thank you, Mr. Stephens. He must be better! Will he be able to go back to work soon?" Lena blurted out excitedly.

"I am not at liberty to tell you anything because the doctors want to speak with you personally," he answered. "All I know is that he is being released. Then," he continued, "I will come personally to pick you up tomorrow, and we will provide you with a room in Chicago so that you will be able to be ready to speak with the doctors the next morning. You may be able to catch the train for home with Paul so that you will be home in time when your children come home from school if all goes well. You needn't worry, however. I have a nurse that will be with the children in the morning, stay the night with them, get them back to school the next morning, and be there when they get off school tomorrow evening. She will stay through another night if it should happen that you don't get home in time. Your children will be well cared for."

Lena began to protest, "They've stayed home by themselves before, but..." She hesitated, "I guess it is different through the night. Thanks, Mr. Stephens. I'll be ready to go in the morning."

Lena was ecstatic! Her husband would be home and soon. She could hardly keep from dancing around the room. That night, she rested comfortably until that dreaded dream again awakened her. She saw her husband in a coffin this time. "Oh, it is just because we were just at Alice's funeral a few months ago. That's all it is. Paul is coming home. He must surely be better." She went back to sleep.

By 7:00 a.m. the following morning, Lena was at the train station, and by 7:30 a.m., she was on the train heading for Chicago. The landscape seemed to go by slowly, and Lena wondered if they would get to Chicago in time for visiting hours. She desperately wanted to see her husband. She saw the beautiful, bountiful fields of corn, oats, and soybeans. She saw the vegetable gardens in glorious colors. She wished that she could have that much land to raise enough food to feed her family. "Dear God," she prayed, "give me back my husband, healthy and sound. I can't live without him." She sobbed quietly.

An older man sitting in the coach seat across the aisle, asked, "Is there anything I can do to help? I noticed that you boarded the train the same time I did. Where are you going?"

He seemed so thoughtful and kind. She looked at him and noticed that he was a tall man. He had a full mustache and piercing eyes. They were full and round and brown. He also spoke with an accent.

"I'm going to Chicago to bring my husband home from the hospital," Lena answered dryly. "I miss him so much. I just hope he is doing well."

"I don't think they would let him come home if he wasn't," the kind gentleman answered.

"That is what I am thinking," answered Lena.

The two of them carried on a nice lively conversation all the way to Chicago. She told him about her family and how they had emigrated from Holland and what a daredevil Paul was and how he stood on his head on the top of the water tower in Parkersburg. "I fear for his life every day," she whispered.

"That is how I always worried about my wife. She was beautiful and liked to go to different places. But we had very little money, and I was afraid of wasting it. Now I am sorry that we didn't go out more. There are lots of house dances that don't cost anything. There are many nice musical groups that go to different houses to play for dances just for the fun of playing. I guess I was an old stick-in-the-mud. Now she is gone, and I can't do anything for her. She died from the flu. It was a couple of years after the flu epidemic of 1918."

As they parted, she hadn't thought to tell him her name. She learned quite a bit about Fred though. Fred Spars seemed to enjoy speaking about his background and learned a bit about hers. She found out that he had come from Oldenburg, Germany, at least five years before she and Paul had immigrated from Holland. She thought, *He seemed nice.*

At the train station in Chicago, she was met by an official from the railroad.

She was taken to the hospital, where she finally saw Paul. He looked drawn and had lost weight. He seemed really glad to see her, and they discussed what the plans were to get him home.

After a brief time at the hospital—because visiting hours were strictly adhered to—she was taken to a nearby hotel. Her accommodations were adequate, and she checked the room, quickly throwing the pillows back, looking for bedbugs or any other disgusting creatures. The room was clean. Thank goodness! She rested well.

The next morning, she was up early to get to the hospital by eight, where she was to meet with the specialists who were treating Paul. Dr. Simmons was very nice. He gave her a chair in which to sit and greeted her with a cheery smile and handshake. She noticed that the hand was firm but seemed a little hesitant at first. Immediately, she felt that there was something amiss.

He began by saying, "Mrs. Viel, your husband has not healed like he should have. His spine seemed to be infected at first. As you know, this was serious enough, but the nerves in his back are all inflamed. He is getting worse, not better, and there is nothing we can do but try to keep him comfortable. At this point, we suspect cancer that we call spider cancer. I am afraid that he may not have very long to live. I am so sorry."

Lena let out a shriek, went limp, and floated into darkness. This was not the news she was expecting to hear—not at all.

Chapter 7

A few minutes passed before Lena came to. Several nurses and doctors were hovering over her when she opened her eyes. "Tell me it isn't true...please tell me it isn't true. I can't lose my husband. I just lost a daughter. My twin boys died in infancy. God couldn't be that cruel!" she yelled. "How can I go on? Please tell me it isn't true! It can't be true!"

"My dear Mrs. Viel, please calm yourself and lower your voice. There are many very ill people in here, and we can't have you carrying on like this," Dr. Simmons stated quickly and firmly. "Nurse Olson, please remain with Mrs. Viel for a while so she can collect her thoughts."

As the group of hospital staff left the room, it was apparent that Lena could not be comforted. Nurse Olson tried her best to get her to calm down, to no avail. Finally, she left Lena with her thoughts for about fifteen minutes. When she came back, she had a hypodermic needle in her hand and said, "Mrs. Viel, if you don't calm yourself, I have been given orders to inject you with this. You will be asleep for quite some time. I understand that you are supposed to go home with your husband to your other children. If I have to give you this"— she held the needle high—"you won't be able to go home today at all. Remember that you have those children at home, and they need a mother. Please try to remember that and give your husband the opportunity to spend his last months at home with you and the children. You will soon have to care for your children by yourself. You need to be strong. I hear that you are Dutch and that you even named your oldest daughter, Wilhelmina, after the queen of Holland. I don't see any of the great determination that the Dutch are supposed to have here in you. Where is that Dutch willpower and willingness to go everywhere just for the sake of exploration and discovering new things? What would your boys say about your carrying on like this?"

Those words seemed to strike Lena's heart in such a way that she straightened up to her full four-foot, ten-inch height, straightened her dress, tucked her hair back into her famous topknot, wiped her eyes with a hankie, and said, "I am ready to take my husband home now. Yes, I am Dutch, and what would the queen say about me right now? She suffered much with all the changes in the country, and the least I can do is hold up, and hold up I will, even if it kills me. I am sorry for my childish behavior. It will never happen again." Lena's pride came to the rescue.

Nurse Olson smiled, held up the needle, and offhandedly remarked, "Then you won't be needing this after all, will you?"

"I certainly will *not*," she said with utmost determination.

Upon their arrival into his room, Paul reached out to his wife and asked, "What's up, my little mother? You look like you've had a rough morning."

He held her in his arms, and she felt safe again.

"Yes, you could say that I have had a bad day, but when we get home, I will fix your favorite meal," she answered bravely.

Dr. Simmons asked rather timidly, "Mrs. Viel, I really need to speak to you privately. I want to give you some instructions as to how you can help your husband at home."

"Very well, Doctor. I will go with you for a few minutes while Paul is preparing to go home." To Paul, she said, "I'll be right back."

She left for about ten minutes and came back with a handful of papers and several prescriptions. She had listened well and had stuffed the papers into her well-worn purse. She was determined to do exactly as the doctor had told her to do. She had a job to do that was very important, and she was determined to do it well—so well that she was convinced she could make Paul well. She would give him good home cooking and lots of tender loving care. She was going to be the best, sweetest, most loving wife and mother she could be. To her, Paul just didn't seem to be that sick.

Chapter 8

*L*ena took very good care of her family. She seldom left the house except to hang the laundry on the line back of the house, go to the garden right out the back door or to the outhouse. When Wilhelmina ("Minnie") was home from school, she spent a great deal of time with her dad. She was helpful in going to the grocery store when something was needed. Sometimes before she left, Paul would give her the sign to pick up some cream cheese, which was his favorite. It was quite expensive, but that was something she could do for her father, even if she got in trouble over it.

The few months moved along much too quickly. Paul deteriorated every day.

It was difficult to watch his body wasting away, and the pain was getting worse as time wore on. Lena wrote letters to Paul's relatives in Illinois, and some of them made the long trip to come and see him. The neighbors were helpful and kind.

Everyone loved Paul, and even in pain, he always had a joke or wisecrack to liven up the conversations. He spoke of his longing for the sea and how he loved climbing the riggings of the sailing ships. This was something he had done since he was a very young man. He loved the feeling of the wind in his face as the ship rode the waves. He never did like the newfangled steamships. The old cap that he always wore was the one he had worn aboard ship. He had it handy at all times, and he set it on his head in a cocky tilt to the left side. As he lay in the living room on the old worn couch, he would play with his hat, having it by his side so that when he got better, he wouldn't forget how to put it on his head, just right.

Wilhelmina had turned nine in 1924, and early in 1925, Paul died. One evening, he fell asleep and just did not wake up the next morning. Lena was devastated, but she knew just what she had to do. A hearse came and took his body to Parkersburg. She made arrangements to buy a cemetery lot there in the same cemetery where Alice was. She arranged to have the lot big enough for her as well. The same church and pastor did the funeral. The railroad helped with the funeral arrangements, as did some of the relatives.

When she arrived at the church, she noticed there was some sort of commotion. Some of Paul's fellow workers had come to the funeral but were not allowed into the church. Lena and Paul and the children never gave a thought to the fact that their friends were "colored," as they were called at that time. Furious to learn that her friends were not allowed to come inside simply because of the color of their skin, Lena stood up, marched down the aisle from her front-row seat, and gave such a dressing down to the pastor that ultimately her friends were allowed to sit in the back. This was the first time that Lena or the children had ever experienced racial discrimination. The term "racist" was not yet coined, but Wilhelmina knew something was very wrong about the way her friends were being treated.

After the funeral, Lena asked the undertaker where Alice was buried. She was led to a fence, and somewhere there, her body had been placed. No marker, nothing. It was where they buried people that had no money. Here Lena and Paul both had thought the church had taken care of everything, but now she discovered that they had not. With this new realization, Lena knew it would be the last time she would ever have anything to do with the church in Parkersburg again. At least she could have been told! Lena would never again see the pastor or any of her fellow members. She was done with it all. In Waterloo, they had a different group of friends and attended no church in that city. They had always thought of the church in Parkersburg as "their" church, even though they had no means of going the 25 miles or so to get there. It wasn't that they didn't want to attend, but they had no car in which to get there. The trains ran, and although they had privileged fares, it still cost money, and they did not want to owe anyone anything.

Lena went home to her little house on Cottage Street. After Paul's death, she didn't know how to go on but began taking in laundry to try to pay expenses. Things were not going well for her. The older boys, George and John, went through Grant School and Junior High and soon decided that they needed to work to help out.

They tried to get work, but it was very difficult to come by. They really liked it when a carnival or circus would come to town because they loved working on the midway where they could entice the customers with their polished speeches. As Ray grew, he especially enjoyed being a barker on the midway. Ironically, in his later years, he became a preacher.

Wilhelmina had many bouts with illnesses as she grew up. She had pneumonia shortly after her dad died. She was hospitalized with a tonsillectomy and removal of adenoids, removal of an abscess behind her right ear, and she also had what was called inflammatory rheumatism, now known as rheumatic fever, which left her with a damaged heart. Of course, all the children had the usual children's diseases, as well as Scarlet fever.

However, even though poor, Wilhelmina did have a number of opportunities as she grew up. Several of her teachers realized her competence in many areas and offered her opportunities in the arts. She took piano lessons, dance lessons, especially tap and Irish dances, and she was excellent at debate. She could recite the works of Shakespeare, Longfellow, the Declaration of Independence, the Gettysburg Address, among the many other important and timeless writings that she enjoyed memorizing. It seemed that she really reveled in the written word, and, of course, she also loved music. As Minnie matured, she took to the Charleston like a pro—how she loved to dance!

A couple of years after Paul's death and when it seemed to Lena that the rest of her life would be nothing but drudgery, things began to change. As she went to the railroad office one day to pick up her small widow's pension, she happened upon Fred Spars and recognized him immediately. He asked how she was doing, and their conversation came as easily as it had on that train ride several years before. It was as if she had known him all her life. She remembered his kindness and again thanked him for his concern.

The last thing he asked was "Would it be all right if I come to call and meet your children? Since my wife's death, I have been so lonely for some company."

At first, Lena was taken aback by his boldness but was surprised at herself when she said quite assuredly, "Yes, I think I would like that very much. I really haven't had much adult company in a very long time." She found herself blushing. Her nervousness showed when she adjusted her topknot several times.

"How about this Sunday afternoon? I can be there about 2:00 p.m. I'll see you then if you have no objections," he declared assuredly.

Lena hesitated but heard herself say, "See you then."

As she walked home, she thought, *Oh my Lord, what have I gotten myself into?* She was angry at herself, at first, for agreeing to such a thing but was surprised when she found herself humming and almost skipping all the way home.

Chapter 9

*F*red continued to come over occasionally on Sunday afternoons. Soon Lena began to include him in the evening meal. He always said grace when they sat down to eat. It was always in High German, as was the custom, and the children did not understand any of it.

All seemed tranquil, at first, and it seemed to be a nice arrangement. The children, however, began to resent Fred being there. They didn't realize that Lena enjoyed seeing him. She knew that she really enjoyed Fred's kindness and his company. She hadn't realized that she missed adult conversation as much as she actually did.

One day, Fred came with a tiny box in his hand. Lena was curious to know what he had brought. He was always very much the gentleman and never approached Lena with anything but kindness and concern. *What sort of thoughtful gift could be in that little box?* she wondered. *Hmmm... I'll bet it must be a new Tee Siep*, she thought to herself, judging by the size of it. Fred sweetly handed it to her, and Lena happily opened the box. To her great surprise, she saw that inside were two matching wedding bands. She was rather shocked, to say the least, to realize that Fred was asking her to marry him!

"Fred," she hesitated. "I need a little time to think. We've been friends now for quite some time, but I need to think this through," Lena stammered. "I have supper ready right now. Maybe next week, I'll be able to let you know." After eating a nice meal together, Fred left, all the way home replaying the scene in his mind, hoping that he hadn't been too forward yet optimistic that she might say "yes."

Throughout dinner Lena was distracted, wondering how to approach the children with the possibility of this new life-changing decision. She decided she must talk it over with all the children and see what their opinions would be. She knew that Minnie would not like it at all. Lena knew that she had a special bond with her father. She had many of his mannerisms, and the two of them could almost read each other's thoughts. This would be her biggest challenge: Minnie—what would she say or do?

When Lena finally mustered the courage to discuss this with the children, there was considerable disagreement.

John was the one to answer first. "Ma, I will support you in whatever you want to do. I have no intention of standing in your way. I have an opportunity to go to Illinois to help Uncle Harm on his farm and make some money, but I have stayed here to help you. If you have a man around here, you really won't need me as much." George piped up with "Ma, I think it would be good for you. Since you have met Fred, you seem more alive. I will soon be old enough to be on my own. So when all of us kids leave home, you won't be alone."

Wilhelmina, who adored her father, almost yelled, "No, Ma, no! You are betraying Dad. How can you even think of marrying anyone else? How can you? How can you?" She was sobbing as she fled the house. All she could think of was "No one can ever take Daddy's place. What is wrong with her? I know she can't love him. Something else must be the reason. I will never let anyone take my daddy's place! I swear!"

As the door slammed behind Minnie, her younger brother Ray said, "I agree to anything you want to do, Mom." He turned to Lena, hugged her, and whispered, "Do what you think is best for the whole family."

Verna, who was the youngest now that Alice was gone, put her two cents' worth in by saying, "You know I loved my daddy and miss him too, but it would really be nice to have Fred around more. He always talks with me, and all I really remember of Daddy is that he was sick. Before he was sick, he was fun, but he is gone now." Verna began to cry.

Lena knew that if she married Fred, her life would be so much easier. He owned a house on Oneida Street that was larger than the little house she was renting on Cottage Street. Fred was older and more mature than Paul was. His children were all grown and out of the house. She would not have a thing to worry about if she married Fred. Her hours and hours of washing clothes for other people on the washboard would be over. Sometimes, her hands bled after she was finished. She would say, "I don't know how some families can dirty so many clothes. They must change clothes every day. Now if Martha would wear an apron like I do, she could cut down the number of clothes she makes dirty," Lena muttered as she worked.

After one of those backbreaking days doing that huge pile of laundry for Martha—who sometimes did not pay her what was agreed upon—as well as another family's laundry and still having to do her own family's laundry, she made up her mind. She would marry Fred. She knew she had already lived her dream with the love of her life, and she was glad that she had experienced that degree of happiness. Now she would also have some security. She would never be haunted by the fear of losing him like she was with Paul. She was not really in love with Fred, but he was good, kind, and hardworking. She vowed to be a good wife to him. She made up her mind, and she would tell Fred on Sunday.

She left to try to find Minnie and knew just where to look. The Sullivans' house was only just a few houses away.

Chapter 10

When Fred arrived the next Sunday, Lena gave him the answer he had been hoping for. She was honest with him about the fact that she would never love him like she did Paul, but she thought they could have a good life together. The next week, they had their blood tests, went to the courthouse, and in a simple fashion, were married by a judge.

Lena had a special meal ready for the family a few days later to celebrate. The next step was moving into the house on Oneida. Everyone was satisfied with the arrangement except Wilhelmina. She hated the whole situation. She was now fourteen. She tried everything to make life complicated. About six months later, Lena was not feeling at all well. Wilhelmina needed to pick up the slack. Although Lena still did the cooking, Wilhelmina had to do everything else.

After visiting the doctor, Lena came home with the unexpected news that she was pregnant. Wilhelmina flew off the handle and yelled, "How could you, Ma, how could you!"

Lena tried to reason with her and said, "Honey, I'm married now, and that is part of being married."

It was a very difficult pregnancy because Lena was forty-two years old by then. She needed complete bed rest during the last six months. This, of course, meant that Minnie had even more to do. She now had to cook in addition to everything she was already doing. She resented every bit of it. She blamed Fred for everything.

One day, when the boys were not in the house, Fred was working, and Verna was busy with her schoolwork, Lena called to Wilhelmina, "Minnie, come sit with me. I need to have a talk with you. I know that you resent my being married to anyone but your dad. I understand your feelings, but don't you realize that we are now able to have things a little easier? Fred has tried his best to earn your trust. You are not even trying to get along with him."

Minnie shot back, "Yeah, easier for you, maybe, but not for me. I hate him! You didn't even remember my birthday!" She was thinking of her fifteenth birthday when they were in the midst of all the new changes. All she got was a "happy birthday" from the family, no special meal or anything. Of course, there were never any gifts because there was never any money.

Lena finally said, "This is the situation now, and you have to live with it. If you don't, you could make some big mistakes in your life. Please make your peace with this." Minnie left the room.

When the new baby girl was born, Lena named her Pauline, after her first husband. Fred was content with it because he knew in his heart that he really loved Lena even though he knew his wife would never really love him.

Minnie helped take care of Pauline, and she loved her, mainly because she had her father's name. But she would never say she was her sister. She would always refer to her as her half sister Pauline.

Not long after, George announced that he was moving to Illinois. It wasn't that he didn't want to live with his mother. He was just ready to start making a life for himself. Since Lena now had security, he felt that he was no longer needed as much. As Lena watched him leave, her heart was heavy because he looked just like his dad. She would look at her son and see Paul in everything he did. He also had that little lisp, just like his dad.

When Wilhelmina began attending East High School, she wasn't very good at coming home on time. She was now in her sophomore year and getting more and more independent. She would sometimes stay out late at night. Minnie had found her niche. She loved to dance, and she went to house dances every chance she got. She found friends there who also loved the music.

One night, while at a dance at the Brown Derby Ballroom in downtown Waterloo, she became fascinated with a wonderful accordion player. Not only could he play the accordion, but he played a mean harmonica as well. He would create the beat on the lower notes as he was playing the melody on the higher ones. Minnie had never heard anything like it. He was also an excellent singer with a high, crystal clear voice that sounded pure and beautiful—like listening to the sound of a delicate waterfall. He was short—about 5 feet, 8 inches—and he was startlingly handsome. He had jet-black hair and shiny blue eyes. She went out on the floor to dance so she could get a better look. Minnie could always find someone to dance with her. She had just turned sixteen in September, and this was the New Year's Eve celebration.

Paul had been eyeing this young lady from the time she walked in the door that night and was completely smitten by the slim, beautiful girl with short blond hair who seemed to be having so much fun dancing to his music. Her loose, silky flapper-style dress flowed as she moved, clinging in all the right places at the exact right time to the music. She could tap dance to the faster songs in a way he had never seen before. Paul became so involved in watching her that he even forgot the words to one of his songs—something which had never happened in all the hundreds of times he had sung that song before.

His band consisted of a guitar player and a fiddle player, with Paul on the accordion, harmonica, and vocals. They had wanted to play the Brown Derby for quite some time, but in those days, Parkersburg was a long drive from Waterloo. This was the "hopping-est" place around, and the money was good, so they were thrilled to finally be playing there.

After their second set that night, Paul finally found the courage to try to approach this intriguing young woman. He made up the lame excuse that he needed a break, and as soon as he put his instrument down, he made a beeline over to Minnie. He was shaking like a schoolboy meeting his first love and barely able to even speak. His nerves caused him to accidentally slip into his native tongue. To his great surprise, she answered back in the same language!

When he introduced himself as Paul, she could hardly believe it. He had the same name as her dad, whom she had loved so dearly, and Paul also seemed to be a lot of fun—just like her dad. He even spoke the same Low German Platt that she had learned from her parents, and Paul spoke with an accent similar to her dad's. All this seemed to be a good omen.

"My name is Wilhelmina Viel, but you can call me Minnie," she said. Before she had a chance to say much more, Paul was called back to the stage.

Toward the end of the evening, Paul took off his accordion and asked the others in the band to continue playing so that he could ask Minnie to dance. Oh, how he could dance! He was light on his feet too. He asked her a little about herself, and she told him everything she could in that short time. He was so easy to talk to. She told him about her father and her situation at home. She told him about not being happy with her mother remarrying and how she hated it. She didn't seem to be able to stop talking to him.

Finally, the evening drew to a close, and as he turned to leave, he asked her if she lived nearby. When she answered "yes," he offered to walk her home, and she eagerly accepted his offer, adding, "Then I'll stay so that we can walk together and continue our conversation after you are finished here." She noticed him singing and humming while he worked on packing up his gear.

As they walked toward Minnie's house that night, they laughed and talked as if they had already known each other for years. Though the evening was cold, neither one of them noticed. Approaching her house, Paul asked if he could meet her after school sometime so that they could get to know each other better. She happily answered, "Yes."

Paul had always said he would never marry. He was already thirty-six years old by this time—quite "old" for someone to still be single in those days. Though Minnie was only sixteen, this was not considered to be "too young" to get married in the early part of the twentieth century. Even though it was not common for a man to marry a girl less than half his age, it was certainly not unheard of. And this girl was special. She was so different from the other American girls Paul had met, that he was already beginning to wonder about a possible future with Minnie. There just seemed to be such a spark between them.

Minnie came home singing that night. She had feelings that she didn't understand.

Paul kept his promise that he would meet her and walk her home from school, and when they reached her house, he told her where he would be playing next and invited her to come. She accepted the invitation and looked forward to listening and dancing to his music again. But most of all, she looked forward to seeing *him* again. Week after week, Paul would invite Minnie to come hear him play, and every time, she would gladly accept the invitation.

As they began to get to know each other, he revealed that he lived with his mother in Parkersburg and that he had owned a farm near there. He had lost everything in the crash of 1929 and could possibly have made it had all his hogs not died of cholera. Now he was taking a job with a road construction crew where he would do a lot of traveling. He could make quite a bit of money as their dynamite man.

This seemed like an exciting life to Minnie. Their family had moved many times following the railroad, so it didn't seem to her to be anything but exciting. *Wow! He's a dynamite man!* she thought. It had never even occurred to her before that dynamite was really all that important.

She finally learned that his last name was Adelmund. She remembered that Lena had not spoken well of the Adelmunds in Parkersburg. Even though she found out that he really was the Paul Adelmund who played music in the bar in Parkersburg and that he was thirty-six years old, she was determined to marry him. He had not married because he said that he had not found the right woman yet.

"Wow, wouldn't that be something! I'd leave home to be with someone Ma doesn't like at all even though she doesn't know him. Ha ha. Wouldn't that be a doozy?"

Only three months later, Minnie married Paul Adelmund. Lena had to sign so that Minnie could marry because of her young age. It was difficult for Lena, but she knew how stubborn Minnie was, and she was afraid of losing her daughter, so she reluctantly signed. Lena and Fred went with them to the Walnut Street Baptist Church rectory, where the minister was concerned about the age difference but performed the ceremony as requested.

That was March 15, 1931.

Minnie went to live in Parkersburg with Paul. In the beginning, she and Paul lived upstairs with his mother, Alice Adelmund. His father, Abbo, had passed away in 1930. She did not like being there when Paul was gone, and he was trying to arrange things so that she could go with him on his road construction job, which Paul called "on the grade." They would be staying in tents, but there was a large dining tent where the women worked on cooking and feeding the crew.

It didn't take long before Minnie and Paul had a little house on wheels that they would take with them. It was a nomad's life. By the time winter was upon them, Paul had enough money to buy a lot on which to place the trailer house in Parkersburg, at least for the duration of the winter. The lot he bought was right across the street from his brother's family. His brother Abbo was older than Paul. He and his wife Lena had married in Germany and came to this country with their first child—a daughter named Verbena. Abbo and Lena were the first to come to the United States. Some of the younger boys of the family—Nann, Harm, Joe, Bill, and Paul's parents, Abbo and Alice Adelmund—immigrated a few years later.

The situation in Germany at that time was bleak. WWI had taken a great toll. When the armistice in November of 1918 was signed, the heavy losses Germany experienced made life very difficult for everyone. The war had just begun when the Adelmunds sold their property in Rechtsupweg, North Germany, and followed their oldest son Abbo to America, as Alice couldn't live without being close to her firstborn.

They bought a house close to the railroad tracks as soon as they arrived and settled in quickly because most of the people in Parkersburg spoke Platt (Low German), which was also their mother tongue. Low German is the language of the lowlands of Germany and the low countries of Europe, whereas High German, which is the official language of Germany, is called High German because it is the language of the highlands of Germany. High German is also the official language of Austria. Platt is a spoken language only.

There had been twelve children in the family. There were two girls who remained in Germany, a set of twins who died in infancy and a son, Jacob, who was killed in battle in the First World War on the side of Germany. It was customary to have the seventh son in the family have the name of the Kaiser, who at the time was named Wilhelm, so, of course, there was a Wilhelm in the family. It was changed to Bill when he arrived in the States. This was the family into which Minnie married.

She was sixteen, and her home base was Paul's mother's house. That first summer on the grade was very trying for her. She had never even camped before, so much of the time, she was either in her own living quarters or in the dining tent. If the company finished a job and circumstances called for time off—for example, if there was too much rain and the site needed time to dry out some—the group had time off but with no pay, of course. This meant that Minnie had to live with Paul's mother until work began again. Even though the work and atmosphere were rough, Minnie liked being alone with her husband. She really enjoyed his company. He always had his harmonica in his shirt pocket, along with the dynamite caps, his pipe, and matches.

Sometimes, the fire in the pipe was not quite out when he stuck it into his shirt pocket. He thought nothing of it because he knew how to use dynamite with such accuracy that he could place dynamite under a rock in such a way that the rock would land exactly where he told everyone it would.

Paul's responsibility was to not only be able to use dynamite with accuracy but also he was to be able to account for every stick, where it was used and why. Paul and Minnie always slept with boxes of dynamite under their bed. That way, he knew it was safe and secure. This was common practice even after the two oldest children were born.

Paul seemed so much like Minnie's father because he was daring and had no fear of anyone. Minnie trusted him and knew instinctively that she was safe with him around. This Paul also could stand on his hands and stand on his head. The big difference was that her father had no fear of heights, but her husband was definitely afraid of heights. However, he had no fear of digging a hole in the earth and going down into it no matter how deep.

This is how they lived from 1931 until 1934. The depression was beginning to lift after Franklin Roosevelt took office as president of the United States in 1933. Paul had a great deal of work. He was a hard worker. He was personable, and everyone liked him.

Minnie was now pregnant for the first time, and in January 1934, she gave birth to a blond-haired, blue-eyed daughter and named her Pauline Alice. It had been customary in Germany to name the firstborn after a parent of the father of the child. Minnie chose Pauline after her husband and her dad and Alice after Paul's mother. This satisfied the requirement. Although she was born in the US, she understood how these things worked because she was a first-generation American.

Now that she was a mother, of course, following the construction company was no longer a viable option, so Minnie stayed in the little trailer on the lot Paul had purchased. First, Paul constructed an outhouse. He dug a deep hole and built a little building over it containing a seat that had two holes carved out of it, which was then placed directly over the large hole in the ground. Although his ability with a saw was minimal and making the round holes in the bench wound up splintery and very out-of-round, it served its purpose. The outhouse was situated to the east of the house about 20 yards away. At night, there was an emergency chamber pot that was used.

Paul dug a garden and turned over the soil by hand with a spade. When he had a chance to be home, he planted the garden and kept it weeded. Minnie also helped keep it weeded. She learned to can vegetables, and Paul dug a storm cellar for protection in the Iowa tornado season with a place to keep vegetables such as potatoes, carrots, cabbages, and more for consumption during the winter months.

In 1936, another daughter was born. She was very small and was covered with black hair. This was a sign of prematurity, but Minnie didn't know that. She was not happy with the look of this child. Pauline was fair and chubby, and now this child was tiny, skinny, and dark. Not only that, but she could not tolerate milk. Lena had come to help Minnie during her convalescence, so she cooked up some oatmeal, strained it, and gave the baby oatmeal water. This seemed to work because the baby was happy and healthy. In those days, women were to stay in bed for ten days after giving birth. Lena stayed for two weeks. Fred, Verna, and Ray took care of Pauline at the house in Waterloo, so Lena felt that she could come and help Minnie.

By now, Paul had acquired a one-room house that he attached to the existing trailer. He made it into a living and dining room. Lena slept on the couch in the living room. Paul, Minnie, and the two girls slept together in one bedroom. There was a good reason for that. They needed to keep warm in winter, and there was no other place. Paul had dug a well, and the water pail would be filled then placed on the table in the dining room. In winter, it froze solid. Minnie would stoke up the coal and woodstove and set the pail on the stove to thaw out. Sometimes in winter, the snow would come in through the cracks between the two buildings because Paul was not very good at doing any kind of building. This is what Minnie's life was like during the Depression.

Although Paul had bought an acre lot close to the cemetery across town, it was not feasible to build on it at that time for two reasons: 1) it was a bog because it was at the lower end of a hill where water gathered, and 2) he could not afford to build yet. When it came to digging and understanding the fall in land, Paul was an expert. But it would take time to remedy these challenges.

Paul knew that considerable fill was needed, and he knew just how to get it. The cemetery needed a gravedigger, and it was arranged that since there would always be extra soil leftover because the coffin and vault took up several cubic feet of space, he used the extra soil as fill for his new lot. It was a good arrangement. He always had extra jobs along with his regular job. He still played music as well. This was how Minnie and Paul got along. It was a difficult life, but they were happy together. Paul absolutely adored Minnie, and he showed that love by taking a cup of coffee to her bed every morning when he was home. He would never wake her up in the morning without a cup of coffee in his hand. It was made just like she liked it, with a little sugar and milk. This was evaporated milk in a can. There were two holes made in the top as close to the edge as possible on opposite sides of the can, popped in there with an ice pick.

Chapter 11

$\mathcal{A}$s all these things were happening with Minnie, Florence grew to be a lovely young woman. She had everything she wanted, and she would soon graduate from high school. She was one of very few girls in Hamlet who actually was able to graduate. Most parents of girls didn't see the need for high school. It was generally assumed that they would get married and would never be able to get any kind of job that would pay anything anyway. To most young women at that time, going to high school was not an option. Women were expected to marry.

Florence took typing, shorthand, and accounting in the hopes that she would be able to secure a job that might at least give her something more than just the very lowest paying jobs that were delegated to women. She might be able to be a secretary or something like that. She was concerned that her parents, being older, may not live very long, and she wanted to be able to help.

As she was walking home one day during the last month of her senior year, she decided to stop at the little restaurant in the hotel to buy a five-cent lemonade. It was already hot this year by the end of May. She would soon graduate, and she was thinking about what she would do. She felt an obligation to be at home to help Ruby and Josiah, yet she also wanted to have a job. She was thinking about that when she heard a deep male voice saying, "What's a beautiful girl like you doing in a place like this?"

She turned around to see a six-foot blond man standing there. He had just walked in behind her. He had piercing blue eyes and a small mustache, and he was a bit disheveled looking and a little dirty like he hadn't taken a bath in a while. He had a captivating smile that seemed to stretch beyond his prominent chin, which had a dimple in it, square in the center. He had a twinkle in his eye. From Florence's standpoint, he was personable and quite bold.

Flora, the waitress in the restaurant, came out with "Don't pay him no mind, Florence, he flirts with everybody. This guy comes in about once a month on his way to Indianapolis. He's a truck driver, and I'm sure you have been warned about truck drivers."

Florence turned to face the man and said quite sweetly, "I've never met a truck driver before, and I've never been to Indianapolis. I'd really like to go there someday."

"Hello, Florence. That is your name, isn't it? My name is Chuck Miller. I've been driving truck for the last five years, and I've never seen anyone as pretty as you."

Florence blushed, adjusted her frock, and pushed her dark hair back over her shoulder. "Gee, thanks. I would really like to see your big truck. Could I look at it?" she stammered as she finished her lemonade. She always wondered what those big trucks looked like up close. She couldn't think of anything else to say. She had never thought about the people who drove trucks before and had no knowledge of them. She didn't know what Flora was talking about.

"Sure, take a look across the street and around the corner. You will see it sitting there. I'm hauling a load from Waterloo, Iowa, to Indianapolis. It's a long way, and it is very tiring. I will be staying in the hotel overnight. Help yourself and take a look. It's the big green and yellow one with a deer logo on it. Oh hell, it's the only one out there" came the reply.

"I will and thanks," she answered, and as she was leaving, she yelled over her shoulder, "Bye Flora, maybe I'll see you tomorrow."

"Hey, that's funny. She hardly ever comes in," Flora muttered under her breath.

As Florence looked for the truck, she was curious about what Flora had said about truck drivers. When she saw the huge truck, she thought about the noise on Highway 30 that she had heard many times and the trucks whizzing by, but when she saw one up close, she marveled at the size of it. "How can anyone control something like that?" she mused.

She found herself skipping along home, her long dark hair bouncing and glistening in the afternoon sun, like a beautiful thoroughbred stallion galloping in the breeze with his mane flowing like ripples in a stream, rushing freely on its way to the ocean.

As she walked into the kitchen, Ruby asked, "What's got you in such a good mood, honey?"

"Gee, I don't know. I'm just happy, I guess. I'll be graduating in two weeks, and I know my grades are good. I can't wait to have my diploma in my hands. It will be a reward for all my hard work. Thanks to you, Mom, because I know Dad doesn't think it's necessary for a girl to graduate from high school, but I know you wanted more for me than you had. Thanks for the opportunity. I'll always love you for it." Florence's voice trailed off as she hugged her mom.

The next morning, as Florence walked to school, she noticed the big green and yellow truck was still parked along the street, and she wondered if Chuck Miller was still sleeping. But as she peeked through the window of the little restaurant, she noticed that he was sitting at the counter wolfing down bacon, eggs, and hash browns. It seemed that he was freshened up and had changed clothes. He was wearing a red shirt yesterday, and today, he had on a blue checkered one.

"Well, at least he's not a slob," she told herself. "When he's cleaned up, I'll bet he is a handsome devil."

As he started to turn around, she left quickly so that he wouldn't notice her watching him.

On her way home from school, she stopped by the restaurant again to have some lemonade, and the first thing Flora said was "I noticed you looking in the window this morning. Are you interested in Chuck? He sure is interested in you. Why, he asked me everything he could think of about you. I didn't give him much information about you though. Be careful, sweetie, he's probably got a girl in every town he's ever been in."

Florence downed the fresh lemonade, turned and replied, "Thanks, Flora, I've got to go now. I'll be careful."

"Just be careful of truck drivers!" Flora yelled after her and muttered to herself, "I hope she doesn't get involved with him. I know his kind. I don't trust him with Florence."

As the days went by, Florence began looking for the green truck with the deer on it. Several times she just happened to be going by the restaurant when she saw Chuck and stopped to talk. She found out that he was from Iowa and that he lived with his parents when he was not on the road. He said they lived in a little town called Parkersburg. "Oh heavens," she muttered to herself as she left, "another small town."

After graduation, Florence began looking for work. There just was nothing to be found in her small town. It seemed that no one could use a secretary, bookkeeper, or a clerk.

One day, Flora asked if she would be interested in helping out at the restaurant. Business was picking up, and Flora wanted some time off. She had been working as much as ten hours a day, split shift, which meant that she had to be at work at 6:00 a.m. then go home after the lunch hour and come back for preparation for the dinner hour. It was taking a toll on her, and she needed some relief. She was the sole support for her daughter after her husband went to Canada to learn to fly warplanes. He enlisted to fly for England because he was sure that war was imminent. There were war signals all around, and anyone who became aware of the situation in Europe knew war was very likely. He was hoping to help before war would be brought to America. By now, the lend-lease program was beginning. This program was about making war matériel for the allies. The hope was that if America provided war matériel to those who were in danger of being attacked, maybe they could take care of it by themselves. America was still trying to stay out of the conflict because Americans were sick of war after WWI. The country was full of isolationists who advocated no war for any reason. This was understandable but somewhat foolhardy at this point in time.

As Florence thought it over, she immediately agreed to Flora's request to do the evening shift. She came in at 3:00 p.m. and worked until closing. This could be as late as midnight some nights. There were more people staying at the local hotel since money was becoming a little more prevalent. More people were working these days. The government had a program, the WPA, where people were hired to build parks and recreation facilities all over the country. The TVA project was also in full swing. This was a government project that was building a huge facility to generate electricity for use over a large area of the country. It also created jobs for people who otherwise had no work. The materials that were needed to build these projects also needed to be produced, and the effects were seen everywhere. People were finally getting back to work. The arrangement of Florence helping out at the restaurant was mutually beneficial to both Florence and Flora.

When Florence arrived at work the following Monday, she felt more satisfied now that she had a job. And with Florence's help, Flora could spend more time with her daughter. Another plus for Florence was that Ruby and Josiah were proud of their daughter's ambition. Although she was still seeking clerical work and spoke to customers occasionally about work possibilities, nothing was forthcoming.

Flora liked working at the hotel restaurant not only for what she earned and the food she could take home but also because it was the only place that gave her access to a telephone. The hotel had a phone system, and Flora could receive phone calls at the hotel in the same building that housed the restaurant. All Flora had to do was go out of the restaurant door straight into the hotel where the lobby was situated. The telephone operator would rush right over when Flora got her much-anticipated phone call from her husband each Sunday afternoon just after completing her workday at the restaurant.

Florence seemed to like meeting people, and she got in on many conversations with travelers from all over the country. There were clerical jobs in the larger towns, but she didn't know how she would get there. She didn't know how to drive, and it was discouraged for women to learn. It was considered the man's place. If the family was able to afford a car, the man of the house always drove.

When Florence started working at the restaurant, she was surprised at how much she actually enjoyed the work. She enjoyed the company of the people she met. She enjoyed the travelers who came and stayed a few days just to relax and enjoy the small-town atmosphere. She met many people from Chicago, Illinois, Indianapolis, Indiana, St. Paul, Minnesota, and she served people even from as far away as New York.

She began to be able to discern where people were from simply by the way they spoke. She liked the accent that she heard from people who came from the northeast part of the country. She enjoyed listening to people from the south also, but she didn't like the way some of the people from northern Wisconsin talked through their nose. She thought it sounded somewhat disgusting.

She really did like the work, and the money was also fairly good. The only thing she didn't like was locking up the restaurant after midnight and walking home afterward. At times, Josiah came to pick her up, but he didn't always show up because there were times when he fell asleep in his chair while waiting to pick her up. He worked hard and was always dog-tired after working on the farm all day.

About a month after Florence started working, Chuck Miller came sauntering in. "Hi, where's Flora?" he asked. "What are you doing here?"

"Flora's with her family tonight, and I work here now," she answered. "What'll you have, big guy?"

"What's your special tonight?" he inquired.

"How about having our ham dinner with mashed potatoes and gravy?" she answered. "Everyone seems to like it."

"Okay, sounds good. I'll have a cup of your good coffee with it too," he offered.

Sitting at the counter, he ate hungrily while keeping a running account of where he was headed and how long it would take to get there. He would be continuing on his way and then stay in Indianapolis. He would probably be back tomorrow night and stay the night. He asked Florence to make sure that he had a place to stay the next night. She said she would.

The next day, just as promised, she went to the hotel to make a reservation for Chuck. Lily, the clerk at the hotel, said that there were plenty of rooms available because it was a Wednesday, and there were usually rooms available in the middle of the week. The weekends were the busiest time for the hotel and the restaurant. Florence was satisfied that she had done as she was asked, so she stopped in to see Flora. She wanted to enjoy the usual freshly made lemonade because it was going to be a really hot day. It was already ninety degrees.

When Flora asked why she was in town so early, she answered, "I came in to make sure that Chuck had a room for the night because he said he would be back to stay."

"Isn't that going the extra mile for a stranger?" asked Flora.

"Well, maybe, but he doesn't seem like a stranger to me. It's like I have known him a long time," Florence answered. "It's okay. If I'd have known that there are always rooms in the middle of the week, I wouldn't have bothered. I'm glad I know that now, if anyone else asks." Then Florence turned on her new heels that she had just bought at Randolph's shoe store and left. It was the first time she ever wore heels this high.

"Oh my goodness," Flora said to herself as she watched Florence hobble down the street. "I think I have opened a kettle of worms. I hope she watches herself."

Chapter 12

When Chuck Miller came to town on Wednesday evening, he stopped at the restaurant first and asked Florence if she had reserved a room for him, and she told him that she had. He said he would be back after cleaning up a bit, then left, and checked in at the hotel.

About two hours later, he came in again, and it was plain that he had gone to the tavern down the street first. He really didn't smell very good although he cleaned up pretty well and looked really nice.

Florence served him but didn't spend much time with small talk. She wanted to get some coffee in him so he could be a little more civil. He used some words she had never heard in her life before and didn't even know what they meant. She politely asked him to clean up his mouth because there were families in the restaurant who didn't want to hear what he had to say.

He finally settled down and ate pretty much in silence after realizing that he had revealed a bit of the worst part of his nature. Florence laid his ugliness to the fact that he had been drinking, and he soon left quietly and went to his room.

A couple of hours later, he banged on the restaurant door leading to the outside. This entrance was only used by Florence when she left at night because she had a key to that door. The door to the hotel lobby was easily locked from the inside. While she was cleaning up before going home, she locked herself in. Florence was almost ready to go home. "Please go away! I'm not open at this hour! I'm just finishing up!" she yelled.

"I need to talk to you, Florence!" he yelled.

Someone opened the window on the second floor of the hotel and yelled, "Shut up and go away! We need our rest! For God's sake, Florence, let him in so we can all go to sleep."

"Florence, open the door!" yelled Chuck.

Florence opened the door and said, "Shush, people are trying to sleep. Go to your room and go to bed. I don't want to talk to you. Just go away. Go sleep it off."

"But I love you, Florence. I can't do this anymore. The only reason I come to this hotel is because I can't get you off my mind. I think of you constantly. I want you so bad, and I need you. Please don't send me away."

He pleaded, and he started to cry. Against her better judgment, she let him in and sat him down in one of the booths toward the back. She turned off all the lights and only left the night light on, as she was instructed to do. She locked up the cash register and took off her apron. The side door to the outside was how she left at night, and she fully intended to leave as soon as possible. She hoped that her father would be coming soon to pick her up.

She knew that she did think of Chuck more than she wanted to admit, and she knew that the real reason she went to work here was to get to see him when he came to town. She had always been drawn to Chuck and had been curious about the outside world. This just might be her chance to get to see some of it. Little did she know that this was an experienced ladies' man, and he knew how to manipulate women. He had little or no respect for them, and he was only out to use them. He was especially drawn to young women who had no experience with men. He would use anything to get a young woman to bed, no matter what it took. He would promise anything and go to any length to get what he was after.

Chuck was not what he seemed. Florence was his goal, and he would ruin her. This night would change her life forever—and not in a good way. This was going to be the beginning of Florence's war. She was naive, and just like the United States, when Pearl Harbor was bombed, her naivete would be her downfall.

Chapter 13

A brisk wind was coming up from the west, which meant a storm was coming momentarily. Lightning started shooting across the sky, lighting up the whole room. Thunder began with a low rumble, and it crescendoed into the booming sound of a tympani roll before the sharp crack of a cowboy's whip.

"Chuck," Florence began, "I really have to get home. The storm will be hitting soon. I thought my dad would be here before this, but I guess I have to walk home. It's a couple of miles from here. If I were allowed to drive, I could come and go whenever I wanted to. I hate it that women are supposed to have a man drive them everywhere. I know that I could learn easily. I think it is a ruse to keep women at home so we can't go anywhere by ourselves, and it's a way to control us. We are always at the mercy of men." She had no idea that her statement would be printed on her mind like a giant banner for the rest of her short life.

"Oh, don't worry, I'll take you home if you don't mind riding in my truck," Chuck volunteered just maybe a little too quickly.

"Sure, if you don't mind. You seem to be feeling a little better than you were earlier this evening," Florence replied. "We really have to get going."

They left quickly. The rain began to fall in torrents as they ran through the wetness. It was like running through solid sheets of water as they made their way to the truck. It was difficult for Florence to get into the seat next to Chuck because she had never been in a vehicle that was so high off the ground. As she struggled and wriggled into the now wet seat, she shivered even though she was not that chilly.

The truck roared into life as Chuck fired up the huge engine. She felt the sheer power of it beneath her body as she tried to settle down. She was excited to be in this monstrous piece of machinery. She was soon laughing as they chatted. It was just small talk. She began to feel quite comfortable.

He took a different route toward her house but was heading in the general direction.

As they were nearing her home, Chuck wanted so very much to gather her into his arms and begin kissing her. He stopped the truck and reached for her eagerly. She was totally taken aback and forcefully pushed him away from her.

"What do you think you are doing?" she croaked. "Who do you think you are?"

She was tired and wet and now felt very uncomfortable. She knew she was excited by this particular man, but she was apprehensive and afraid. She had never had these feelings before and had never had anyone this close to her before.

"I'm sorry," he said quietly. "I thought you would really like to experience a real man's kiss. I know I am older than you are, and I know I could teach you how to kiss." To himself, he said, "Among other things."

She felt a little more at ease, and she figured that this might just be her knight in shining armor. He had saved her from the pouring rain, and now she listened to the rain and fell into its rhythm. It seemed to say, "It's okay. It's okay." That song began in her head and reached into her soul.

He nestled close to her, and she felt his warmth, and he kissed her gently as he pulled her closer. She kissed him in return and felt something stirring inside of her that she had never felt before.

Soon he was kissing her wildly and passionately, and she knew she was in deep trouble. She didn't know what to do because she had never been in this position before. She had nowhere to go. She couldn't find the door handle to get out, and he pulled her back toward his body.

She struggled, but her heart wasn't in it. She kept saying, "No, no, I can't do this. I can't let my mom and dad down. It wouldn't be right." Finally, she realized that the struggle was useless because he held her fast, and she couldn't escape.

She also didn't want to get bruised up and bloodied because she didn't want anyone to know how foolish she had been, so she finally stopped struggling and let herself get caught up in the passion of the moment.

When it was all over, she began sobbing so hard that she had difficulty uttering a sound until finally, she moaned, "Please just take me home. I just want to go home."

Chuck tried to comfort her, but she was not to be consoled. "I'm sorry," he murmured, his voice cracking. "I didn't know that you were a virgin. I'm so sorry."

"What did you think I was?" Florence snapped. "You surely knew just from our first kiss that I was totally inexperienced. I never wanted my first time to be like this. I always dreamed that my first time would be with my husband after the wedding. Now I am ruined. Just take me home now, or I will walk from here. I don't care if it is raining. I don't care anymore if I am struck by lightning. I'll never care about anything ever again."

"Please forgive me. I just needed you so bad. I've loved you from the moment I first saw you. You are so beautiful," he apologized. "I am so sorry."

He sounds like he is crying, she thought to herself, *but I don't feel sorry for him. He got what he wanted. I was such a fool to be alone with him. I should never have accepted this ride.*

He got the truck started, and the moment they got to the driveway of the farm, she found the handle and opened the door. Not remembering the height of the vehicle, she literally fell out the door. In the process, she got even wetter and dirty as she fell into a deep mud puddle and lay helplessly on the ground. Chuck got out and tried to help her up, but she pulled away and yelled into the wind, "I hope I will never ever see you again."

She ran to the house and tried to get to her bedroom before Josiah got out of his chair.

"Is that you, Florence, sweetheart?" he asked quietly, so as to not wake Ruby.

"Yeah, it's me, Dad. It is raining, and I am all wet and dirty. I fell into a big mud puddle in the yard. I wish you could have come to get me tonight. The rain is awful, and there is a lot of wind with it. I've never felt so filthy. The lightning and thunder were so bad. I thought for sure that you would be awake to get me tonight." Under her breath, she muttered, "Tonight of all nights."

Josiah said, "I am so sorry, dear, but I put in a really long day, and it is way after midnight. Did I hear a truck of some kind bring you home? It sounded like a semi."

"Yeah, a guy from the restaurant brought me home. I never thought I'd actually get to ride in one of those big rigs. It was some experience, to say the least. That's how I got all muddy. It is so high off the ground that I fell out the door. I misjudged the height of the darn thing. I got my new shoes all messed up."

To herself, she whispered, "Among other things."

Josiah volunteered, "No wonder you are upset, sweetie, but you can get them clean again. I'll help you in the morning. I need to get to bed. Good night. See you tomorrow. Have a good sleep."

She went into her room, filled the washbasin, washed, and scrubbed herself all over. She was trying desperately to wash off the smell and the guilt of what had transpired. She just couldn't seem to restore the feeling of being clean no matter how much she tried to cleanse herself or how much soap she used. In the same washbasin, she washed out her underwear and noticed blood as well as other fluids in them. Then she hung them on the metal bedstead at the foot of her bed.

She dressed in her nightclothes and sat in the chair near the window. She saw the truck in the distance. The rain was still falling, and it swam down the window in little rivulets, in rhythm with the tears falling down her cheeks. She couldn't stem the flow of those tears any more than she could stem the flow of the rain on the window. She knew her life would never be the same again. She felt that her life was over.

Hours later, she fell into bed and cried herself to sleep as quietly as possible. She hoped tomorrow would never come. Thus, began the war of Florence's life.

Chapter 14

It was a couple of weeks later, and Florence still could not get that night out of her mind. She really wanted to forget the whole thing. She wracked her brain to try to comprehend how she could have let herself get tricked into a situation like that.

Although she was young, she knew that things should have been different. She realized that her own passion had caught her unaware. She really thought that she would be able to handle the situation at the time.

One Monday morning, a few weeks later, she came into the restaurant, and as the bacon began to fry, she felt sick to her stomach. She ran to the bathroom and was overcome by waves and waves of nausea. It overtook her to the point that she was sure she was going to die, and when she didn't, she was sorry.

Somehow, she got through the morning. As her shift came to a close and Josiah came to pick her up, she began to feel better. When she arrived home, she went to her room and slept on and off for a couple of hours. When she arose, she felt much better. For several more weeks, Florence struggled to overcome the awful bouts of nausea, yet she didn't seem to be getting any better.

Twice during this period, she discovered that Chuck had been in town but made no effort to see her. She did not want to see him anyway and made certain that she was not working when he came to town so that she would not bump into him anywhere. She felt too sick to see anyone, really. It made her vomit just thinking of him.

The constant flu symptoms went on for several more weeks. One day, her mother took her aside and said, "Florence, if I didn't know better, I would think that you are pregnant. It looks like morning sickness to me. These flu symptoms are not getting better. I think you need to see Dr. Travis."

"Oh my god!" Florence cried, "Oh, Mom! I think maybe I could be pregnant!"

By this time, Florence was wailing, and between sobs, she told the whole sordid story—how Chuck had brought her home, how he held her captive in the semi. Everything came pouring out like a dam breaking. At last, relief came over her as it all came bursting through. Now she wouldn't have to keep her guilty secret any longer. Relief and despair were to be her companions for at least this day. She could always count on her Mom to help her.

"What am I gonna do, Mom? What am I gonna do?" she wailed.

Josiah heard the commotion, came into the kitchen, and asked, "Mother, what is going on? What could possibly be so bad that you are both so upset?"

After Josiah heard everything, he was furious. He was ready to go find Chuck and shoot him on the spot.

The household became embroiled in the turmoil such that nothing seemed right, nor would it ever be again. Florence's parents tried to figure out what they had done wrong in raising her and started to take the blame themselves for the situation. "We should never have let you take that job at the hotel restaurant," Josiah lamented. "I wish I would not have fallen asleep! Why didn't I wake up soon enough to pick you up, especially when it began to rain? I only woke up after you got home. It's my fault. Oh, Florence, I am so sorry."

They all began to talk about their options. The chaos lasted all day. On and on, it went with blame being transferred from one to the other. It was the very worst day they had ever experienced. Even the day of Ruby's accident several years ago was not as chaotic a day as this one. At least then, nobody felt to blame. After a very difficult evening meal, it was decided that they needed to get to bed. They hoped that things would be easier to sort out in the morning. Everyone was totally exhausted and emotionally spent.

As Florence finally fell into a fitful sleep, she became plagued with the scenario of that fateful night, which played over and over again in her nightmares.

The first thing the next morning, the family decided that Florence should see a doctor to determine if Florence was, in fact, actually pregnant. As they drove to town, Florence and Ruby were praying the entire time that Florence was not pregnant, hoping she only had a touch of the flu or some other malady that could be easily treated. As they approached the doctor's office, Josiah said, "I think the next step is to locate Chuck." Florence knew that he was from a small town in Iowa, but that was all she knew about him.

They arrived at Dr. Travis's office and had to wait a few minutes while the doctor worked on another patient who had a broken arm. Apparently, he and a friend had been cutting down a dead tree, and as it came down, it struck his left arm. The tree started to twist, and he used that arm to shield his head. It all happened so fast that he couldn't really explain how it happened.

Florence was getting more and more nervous as she sat and waited. When she was called in, she explained her symptoms, and she told the doctor about what had happened on that fateful night. Ruby was with her the entire time, holding her hand. As Dr. Travis examined Florence, he said, "There is a little bulge in your uterus, and since you have not had your period for a couple of months, I would say the possibility is great that you are pregnant. Someday, maybe, we will be able to tell for sure sooner. If I had an X-ray machine, I'd know, but I don't think that is necessary anyway."

Florence and Ruby knew that all their hopes and dreams for a good life for Florence were over. That was certainly not the life that Ruby had planned for her daughter. She was sick at heart. When they got home, they began to discuss what to do about this unfortunate turn of events. This was something they never dreamed would happen to their only child—at least not this way.

Florence asked quite innocently if there was a way to stop the pregnancy. Ruby asked, "What do you mean?"

Florence answered, "Well, I know that sometimes a baby doesn't really form right, and it comes before it can survive. I know that our neighbor down the road had it happen to her. You know, Mrs. Ryan? I think they call that a miscarriage. Is there any way that we can make that happen to me? Is there anything we can do to make that happen so I don't have to have this baby? I want children but not this way."

"Florence, do you mean abortion?" asked Ruby, totally shocked and appalled at the very thought of such a thing.

"I don't know what it is called, but I am asking," answered Florence.

Ruby began to explain that if something like that even could be done, no real doctor would do it. She explained that their religion would call that murder, and if it were done illegally, in some back alley somewhere, she could die in the process.

Ruby concluded with "You have to get married, Florence, so that your baby will be legitimate and have a father. I think we need to plan for a wedding and a new baby." Ruby didn't realize the battles Florence would face in a forced wedding. All the while, Josiah sat quietly and listened to the conversation. He finally jumped up and suddenly announced, "I'm going to town."

As he went out the door, he yelled, "Don't worry, girls, I am going to fix everything! If I find that bastard, I am going to fix him good."

As he left the house, he grabbed his shotgun, got into the car, and barreled down the road. He was still muttering to himself as he left the yard about how he was going "to take him out."

When Josiah reached the restaurant, he got out of the car, marched inside, and asked Flo every question he could think of about this guy named Chuck. He wanted to know when this SOB might be coming back to town, how he could find out where he lived, what she knew about him, and on and on. Finally, Flo said, "I warned Florence about that guy several times. I just know he is no good. I have lived longer than Florence, and I wanted to give her some advice from my own experiences. You know Florence, she's smart and sassy and doesn't take well to advice. I will tell you that you should be able to find him from the hotel registry. They have to sign before they can get a room, and that includes a home address and the company that they work for. That should give you the information that you need."

"Thanks, Flora, I appreciate your help," Josiah flung back as he went out the door.

He immediately went into the hotel part of the building. He asked the young lady at the counter if he could see the registry. She was not sure that she should allow that. She thought it was infringing on other's rights to remain anonymous. She knew that sometimes when there was a family disturbance, town residents stayed overnight in the hotel, and it was to be kept secret, especially when it was the mayor or town constable.

"Well, young lady, what is your name?" Josiah asked.

She answered, "They call me Marty, but my real name is Martha."

"My, that is a pretty name, and I am pleased to know you. I have seen you before when my wife and I have come in for tea at the restaurant here. My daughter works in the restaurant, and, on her behalf, I am desperate to find someone. The young man's name is Chuck, probably short for Charles, and he is from Iowa. He drives one of those big rigs to Indianapolis and back."

"Oh, you mean Chuck Miller," she countered. "You won't have to look at the register because he has a reservation for this coming weekend. He should be here on Friday evening."

"Well, thank you, Marty. You don't know how happy you have made me," responded Josiah sweetly.

To himself, he muttered, "I guess you can get more cooperation with honey than with vinegar. Yep, you sure can." Louder so that Marty could hear, he said, "I need to think this through and talk with the girls. I think I have a plan."

Returning home, Josiah came in, grinning through the kitchen door. Florence was ready to go to work on the second shift. Josiah laughed and said, "I'll take you to work, even though it is a nice day, and you could enjoy a walk. We need to talk."

As the two of them left, Ruby could finally sit down and think things through. "I am going to have a grandchild," she mused. "Thank you, Lord, for this gift, but I sure wish it could have been different. I don't even know this young man. Help us through this, Lord. I leave it all in your hands. There is nothing I can do. You know best." She opened her Bible and enveloped herself in the calming that the Scriptures always gave her.

In the car, Josiah was asking Florence, "Well, what do you want to do? Do you want to marry this man?"

"I never thought much about it before because I really did want to wait a few years before I would feel comfortable being a wife and mother," answered Florence, adding, "I don't think I even love him, or ever will, because of what he did. I don't feel comfortable with the control he has over me, and I'm sort of scared of him. There is something about him that makes me worried about what he will do next. I have the feeling that he enjoys making women do whatever he wants them to do. I have seen him use his power over women. I really don't know what it is, but it makes me nervous."

Josiah weighed his words carefully and said, "Well, honey, the man should marry you, especially since you are in the family way."

Florence looked into Josiah's eyes and replied, "Dad, let me think about it. Right now, I need to go to work. Thanks for everything. See you later." As she opened the car door and got out, she came back with "Remember, I always said that I wanted a bunch of kids, but I didn't expect it to happen like this."

She had no idea that her desire would never become a reality. Her dream would collapse in her war to come. That night as she drifted off, her nightmare repeated itself. Again, she did her best to get away, and she awoke in a sweat.

Chapter 15

*F*riday morning dawned bright and breezy. It was a day that would be in Florence's mind for the rest of her life. She was anxious and afraid of what the day would bring. She worried that Josiah would do something he would always regret. She knew that the plan was that as soon as Chuck's truck hit town, the three of them would be there to confront him.

About four in the afternoon, they went to the restaurant and had a nice meal. That way, they would be right there when Chuck pulled in to register at the hotel. About an hour later, they heard the sound of the big rig. They all began to rise from the table.

Florence was holding her breath. Josiah reached into his bill-fold, pulled out a ten-dollar bill, laid it on the table, and walked out the door.

As he strode in front of the rig, Chuck got out of the truck and yelled, "Be careful, old man, you might get run over. Of course, nothing would be lost." He snickered at the thought. "I need to talk to you, Chuck," the old man said very politely.

"Who the hell are you? And what makes you think I would want to talk to you, old man?" snarled Chuck.

"Maybe you'll talk to me, the woman who is carrying your child!" yelled Florence. Chuck was taken aback, and Florence continued, "That's my dad, you are confronting, and I resent what you are saying. That is the grandfather of *your child*. Now what do you have to say? Or do you have nothing to say? Come on now, speak up." Florence chided, "Your mouth is open. Either close it or use it."

All Chuck could say was "What the hell are you talking about?"

"Well, maybe we should go inside and talk about this in a mature manner," offered Ruby.

"Who the hell are you?" a surprised Chuck asked as he whirled around to see Ruby behind him.

"I am the grandmother of your child," Ruby growled.

"What child? What do you mean? For God's sake, just leave me be," he whimpered.

Chuck thought he could get on Ruby's good side by acting like he was about to cry. It always worked with women, but it made no difference to Ruby. He wasn't sure what was happening, but he knew he had better listen. Ruby had made it clear that he was not about to be left alone. As long as she was alive, he would never be rid of Ruby. He could just feel it.

Ruby took him by the arm and led him inside. By now, the booth had been bussed, and they all sat down. Ruby laid the options on the table very calmly. "You either marry Florence, or you will be charged with rape. Those are your options," Ruby purred. "The wedding will take place as soon as possible, maybe even tomorrow."

Chuck objected, "How can I be sure that the brat is mine. How do I really know? I don't want to get married. I never have. I sure as hell never wanted any kids."

"You should have thought of that before you took advantage of Florence. She is a good girl, and she is carrying your child," Ruby hissed through clenched teeth. "Now what are you going to do about it?"

At that, Josiah finally had enough, and with clenched fists, he grunted, "I would like to beat the tar out of you. I also have a shotgun in the car, and I should kill you right here. If you try to run away, I will surely shoot you dead as a doornail, I swear. These are your options. You will leave here with a bride or leave here in a pine box. No one will convict me of your murder since you raped my daughter, and now she is pregnant. You are her child's father, and because of that, I have restrained myself, or you would be dead already."

By the time the confrontation was over, Chuck had agreed to marry Florence the next day. On his way back from taking his load to Indianapolis, he would stop to pick up his bride and take her with him back to Iowa.

Josiah was going to take the truck keys from Chuck to ensure that he would have no way out of town but came up with a better idea. The three of them left and went by the constable's office and asked him to make sure that Chuck would not get through town without his bride. The wedding would take place in the morning.

Early the next morning, Chuck was barreling as he came through town, but when he stopped at the stop sign, there was the constable, and he was brought to the hotel. He was given the opportunity to change clothes and freshen up. The constable kept him in sight when Florence and her parents, along with the justice of the peace, came into the room. Peace, however, would never come to Florence.

The sun was shining brightly when, in the lobby of the hotel, Florence became Mrs. Charles Miller. The justice of the peace was kind and very supportive. He reminded Chuck of the responsibilities of marriage. The night before, he had heard the story from Florence and had misgivings but agreed to do the wedding for her sake and the child that was to be born.

Chapter 16

After the ceremony, they all had lunch at the restaurant, and it seemed like the whole town turned up to congratulate the bride and groom. Florence tried to keep an upbeat attitude but was petrified, thinking of what the night would bring.

The day had turned wet and dreary, and after all the greetings, everyone left. Florence just picked at the evening meal. She tried to make it last as long as possible. Then the two of them went upstairs. Their honeymoon night was spent in the room Chuck had previously reserved. Now she was totally alone with him.

It was an awful night for Florence. Being in bed with Chuck was bad enough because she had never tried to sleep with anyone before, not to mention the things that he expected her to do. She tried to accommodate him, but her heart was not in it. She was scared, and she felt alone even with the man who was now her husband. She was as miserable as the dreary day. She knew that she didn't love him. She hoped that she would get used to the things he expected of her.

Chuck dragged her out of bed early in the morning so they could be on the road in time to make it to Waterloo and Parkersburg by nightfall. She wanted to go back to her childhood home to pick up a few of the things she had forgotten. Along with dealing with morning sickness, she was miserable and had difficulty even thinking about the long ride in that bouncy truck. Her earlier romantic ideas of seeing the country in a big truck disintegrated in her mind, like confetti falling to the ground into the mud on a soggy afternoon, behind a canceled parade. Reluctantly, Chuck agreed to take her to the farm, but he was not happy about it. He wanted to get going and soon. He was already late getting the truck back to the company, and he feared that he could be fired.

When she arrived, Ruby knew her beautiful daughter was not happy, as brides were expected to be, but she made sure that she was supportive and pretended that everything was okay. She laughed and joked with Florence to try to cheer her up, and as they pulled out on the highway, Florence could still see her parents waving goodbye. She was still waving, even when she could no longer see them.

Tears were streaming down her cheeks as she waved. She was not sure that she would ever get to see her parents again.

Florence and Chuck were on the road by seven o'clock. Chuck knew that it would be a very long day. The two-lane highways made driving difficult, especially with a semi. The road was very busy, and there was no room to pass the four-wheelers. He was getting more and more agitated because of the slow going. He had very little patience anyway, and Florence heard cursing the likes of which she had never heard before.

As they drove along, Florence was uncomfortable with the entire situation. She understood that Chuck would never have chosen to be married. She really didn't like the idea very much either, but she had no choice in the matter. Her upbringing would not allow her to do anything else. She simply tried to accept that it must be the will of God. After all, she was pregnant with Chuck's child. The one and only time she let anyone get that close to her, and now she would become a mother. She still was ashamed that everything happened as it did, but the deed was now done, and she had to make the best of it. All she could think of, at this point, was that she had to take care of her baby. She knew that she didn't really know how to do that, and she would not have her mother nearby to rely on. She had always depended on her mom when she needed help, and now, in the most desperate time of her life, she would not be able to do that.

"Chuck," she began, "I am sorry that I got pregnant, but the best thing we can do now is to try to give our child a good home. Do you have any plans as to where we are going to live?"

"Well, Florence, I didn't choose this path. I've never wanted to be a husband or a dad, but now that we are in this mess, I promise to try to do my best to get us through this," he said in a placating manner that was not very convincing. "But to answer your question, I don't know where we'll live. But I do know that my parents will be happy that I am finally married and to know that they will soon be grandparents. They've always wanted to be grandparents. I am an only child, and their only chance to be grandparents is through me, so I guess that's the only good I can see in our predicament. They will welcome us into their home, I am sure." That was the most Chuck had really spoken to anyone in particular since the "I do."

"Well, I'll do the best I can to make them feel that I am worthy of their son," Florence answered. "And I do know how to work."

The conversation seemed to be a little more on the bright side as they neared the city of Waterloo where Chuck would leave the truck and then drive on to Parkersburg, another 20 miles west, in his little '31 Chevrolet, which she had never seen. The trip had taken a good twelve hours with as few stops as possible.

The two-lane highway had areas that were still gravel between Waterloo and Parkersburg in 1939. As they left Waterloo, they began discussing the fact that Germany had taken over Austria and that America was fearful that Hitler would conquer the whole world. Little did they know that Poland would be invaded with a new sort of warfare, a Blitzkrieg or "lightning war" in September of 1939. When he did hear the news later, Chuck laughed and burst out with "Holy cow, I suppose America will be in the fight soon, and maybe, just maybe, this baby of ours will keep me out of the draft, if it comes to that. Maybe something good is going to come out of this situation after all."

Florence was appalled that the baby she was carrying only meant to Chuck that it might be a way to stay out of the draft. She began to wonder if he had planned it that way. This thought came to her each time she heard talk of war, which had been going on for quite some time. He certainly seemed to be more civil since he heard the news that war was already beginning in Europe.

Florence already loved her baby. He or she was not an object or a thing that was useful for some selfish goal. To her, she was carrying a person, a new human being whom she loved with all her heart. At that moment, she felt blessed indeed. When she finally did meet her in-laws after arriving in Parkersburg, Mr. and Mrs. Miller were sitting in the living room when Chuck burst in with the news. "Hi, Mom, Pop, meet my new bride. Her name is Florence."

Both faces went ashen, and Chuck's mother fell back into the chair from which she had just risen. There had obviously been no previous warning. "My god, when did that happen? We didn't even know that you were engaged! We didn't even know you had a steady girlfriend!" John Miller exclaimed.

"Well, I didn't, but Florence is pregnant with my kid, and we plan to live here in Parkersburg just as soon as we can find a place," Chuck offered.

"Damn it, Chuck, you never could keep that thing in your pants." John couldn't help but say what he was thinking. "What the hell were you thinking? I can see that she is lovely, but for God's sake, she is still so young." Turning to Florence, he said, "You are a sweet-looking young lady, and I am sure that you are a good person, but I am disappointed in my son. I'm sorry, dear, if I offended you in any way, but he is old enough to know better."

Mary Miller finally found her voice and chimed in, "What? I'm going to be a gramma? When?"

Florence, her voice barely audible, timidly answered, "The doctor said that I am about four months along. I have had terrible morning sickness. It's not just in the morning, but all day long sometimes."

"My dear, I will get you some crackers and milk before you retire to Chuck's old room. That always seems to help, and you need the calcium. If you don't get enough calcium, you will be sacrificing a tooth for each pregnancy," clucked Mary.

Florence and Chuck got to bed late after answering all the questions posed by the Millers about their meeting and about Florence's parents. They asked about the wedding, where it took place, what she wore, who performed the ceremony, and lots of other questions. Chuck and Florence told them everything—except for the fact that it was forced upon them. Before the evening drew to a close, both Mary and John began beaming about the fact that they would have a grandchild.

Florence and Chuck lived upstairs in the little two-story house by the Catholic cemetery for a month. Mary and John began searching for a house for the young couple to rent. As luck would have it, another young couple moved out of a nice little home when the young man joined the Navy because war seemed imminent.

He felt that if he went in soon before the draft came about, he would have a chance to go into the branch of service that he chose.

Gradually, with the help of many of the good people of the small town, Florence and Chuck gathered enough materials and furnishings to rent the house on their own without the help of the Millers. It was on a street that many years later would be named Miners Street. At that time, there were no names of streets. You received and sent mail by going to the post office downtown on the main drag, which consisted of one and a half blocks of stores. You rented a post office box if you had the money. Otherwise, you had to wait until the window was open at certain hours and ask for your mail from the postmaster. The building was always open, so if you had a post office box, you could get your mail at any time. It was secure because there were combination locks on the post office boxes.

Florence and Chuck finally got settled. Chuck still went on his usual route with the truck and kept up with his "extra-curricular" activities. Even when he was in town, he was seldom home, and Florence was lonely much of the time. She spent all her time making her home as nice as she could with little or no money.

Little did Florence know that Chuck's marriage vows meant nothing to him. He still had his women in various places, even in the small town of Parkersburg. There was one in particular who was furious that Chuck was now married. She was older than Chuck, and she owned the restaurant that he often frequented. When he was in town, Chuck would eat at the restaurant with her. Afterwards, the two of them would retire to her house behind the restaurant for some "playtime."

The very next morning, after bringing Florence home with him, he went to the restaurant alone. He wanted to let his lover know that he was married, and he still intended to keep seeing her. In a small town, everyone knows what everybody else is doing, so he knew that he would have to let her know the whole story. Although Etta was furious with him for marrying someone else, she agreed to keep seeing him. She still hoped that one day, he would marry her. She just couldn't help herself. She loved him, and for some odd reason, she needed him.

Florence was oblivious to all that. For half a year, she hardly ever left the house, had no access to a telephone, and she had no friends. Once in a while, she would walk to the store and, of course, had no access to a vehicle of any kind and wouldn't know how to drive it even if she had one. She busied herself with making her home clean, neat, and ready to receive a baby. Her life was not at all what she had envisioned. She missed her parents and her life in Indiana. She rued the day that she met Chuck. She totally concentrated on the life that she was carrying inside her and talked to her baby constantly. This is what she had wanted all her life, and she was happy with just her and her baby. She had no idea that this was the lull before her war began in earnest. She didn't know that she should be preparing for her war—in much the same way that America needed to be preparing for the worst.

Chapter 17

One beautiful day in March, Chuck had left for his run to Chicago and on to Indianapolis, so Florence decided to walk to the post office and store. She had gotten a few dollars from Chuck to buy some groceries and went to the Diamond Brothers Grocery Store. This was the grocery store that had things in bulk.

As Florence entered the store, she saw a young blond woman, obviously pregnant, with two young daughters in tow. The older girl was chubby and blond. The other little girl was very skinny and had jet-black hair. *What a combination*, she thought. She saw that the mother was trying to get her purchases paid for. The little girls were quite well behaved and were trying to help carry the bread and a bag of coffee. The black-haired one was trying so hard not to squeeze the bread. She couldn't seem to stand still, so it was difficult not to hold it tightly. In the end, the bread was crushed in the middle.

When the mother was leaving, Florence came up to her and said, "Hi, my name is Florence. May I help you?"

"Hi, my name is Minnie Adelmund, and these are my two daughters, Pauline and Wilma." The two girls said a bashful "hi." "The older one is named after my dad and my husband, Paul. The younger one is named after me. My given name is Wilhelmina, but I go by Minnie. I was named after the queen of Holland." Minnie held out her hand and shook the hand of a newfound friend.

"Where do you live?" Florence asked.

"Oh, just a block and a half down the street here. We have bought some land on the other side of town where we intend to build a house pretty soon, we hope," Minnie answered. "I really have to get home. Paul will be home for supper, and I have to get it started. You are welcome to come along and rest a bit because you look like you will have your child soon. I'll put the coffee pot on."

Florence was delighted to go with Minnie to help her with her meager sack of groceries but mostly to make a friend. Florence and Minnie hit it off right away. They shared stories about their lives, and before they realized it, the day was gone. All the while, Minnie was putting some food together for her family.

When Paul came home, Minnie introduced him to Florence, and he invited her to stay for supper, especially since her husband was going to be gone for a few days anyway. They all had supper together and enjoyed talking and laughing. It had been a long time since she had laughed like that. It was quite a revelation to Florence to see a family so obviously poor but happily working together. She could see the love that Paul had for Minnie and the sparkle in Minnie's eye as she looked at Paul. Her family in Indiana had a much richer life in material things, but she could feel the respect and caring that this humble home held. In actuality, it was two shacks pushed together. One part was the kitchen and bedroom. The other became the living/dining room. The kitchen/bedroom had actually been the trailer house that they had when Paul worked on the grade where he was the dynamite expert. The floors between the two were not at the same level. In winter, where the two shacks came together, snow would actually blow through and form a snowbank on the floor between where the table stood, and the kitchen wall started. The living/ dining room had a dirt floor at this stage. Later, some plywood was added, which made it considerably warmer and homey. It also made the step up to the kitchen lower. It did not, however, totally fix the snowbank situation.

Looking at this humble couple, Florence realized that her mom, Ruby, and her dad, Josiah, looked at each other, just like Paul and Minnie did. It was something that she knew she didn't have with Chuck, nor would she ever have.

As the evening wore on, Paul offered to take Florence home. He took her home in the wrecker that he had with him from Kyle's

Chevrolet Garage, where he worked part-time. Paul made sure that she was in her house and that everything was secure before he left. Paul wished Florence a good night and went home and crawled into bed. He worked hard digging ditches by hand for a living, and he was tired. His work for the garage consisted of tearing junk cars apart so that repair parts could be salvaged.

Minnie finished the cleanup with the help of her two little girls, and they all snuggled in for the night together in the same double bed.

Florence went to sleep that night, thankful that she had a friend in this unfamiliar, yet seemingly friendly little town.

Chapter 18

*I*t was late morning when she awoke to the sound of banging. Someone was banging on the door. She was almost afraid to open it until she looked out to see who was there. It was Mary and John checking up on her. They were concerned because they had come to the house the evening before and found her gone.

She invited them in and offered to make them a cup of coffee. She knew how it was done because she learned that in the little restaurant she had worked in before she left Indiana. She didn't usually make coffee because Chuck stopped at the restaurant for breakfast.

She told them about how she had met Minnie and Paul and their two little girls. John did not seem happy that she had met them. He hesitated as he told how Minnie's dad had stood on his head on the water tower for fifty dollars and that the Adelmunds were tough. They used to fight a lot, and it is said that they could lick anyone in town. On the other hand, since Paul married Minnie, he had settled down more. Also, he said that there is music in "those Adelmunds."

John ended his little story with "Every Saturday night, Paul and those two little girls go into the Welcome Inn Beer Hall and play music and sing. Paul plays the old-style button accordion and harmonica, and they all sing. The older girl can even sing harmony while the little one sings the melody. When all three of them sing, it is just beautiful. We two go there just to hear them make music. Minnie used to sing, but she was stricken with a terrible infection of some kind and can no longer sing well. People have said she could really sing before that."

Just before they left, Mary said, "Just to give you a little more information, if you will notice that Paul has a crooked nose. He has a good-sized nose to start with, but you can tell that it is bent to one side. That is because he was in a fight, and he tried to pull it straight but didn't get it exactly right. That guy has a twinkle in his eye all the time. He is always happy and would give you the shirt off his back if he thought you needed it worse than he does. His honor means everything to him. If he says he'll do something, he will keep his word. You can trust him with your life. Just make sure that you don't cross him."

Just as Mary was about to go out the door, Florence let out a yell and bent over in pain.

"Oh, I think I might be going into labor. I didn't sleep well because I had these little twinges most of the night. It is much more than little twinges now. I think I'd like you to stay with me for a while, Mary. I don't expect Chuck to be here until at least tomorrow night. I don't think I should be alone."

Mary jumped at the chance to stay with Florence. John went to Dr. Bruechardt's office to inform him that they thought Florence was in labor.

Florence was on the bed when the doctor arrived. Mary was tending her.

The doctor said that he had to make a call nearby and that he would be back in plenty of time to deliver the baby.

As Florence lay there, she felt sorry for Mary and John. They deserved better than she could give their son. She hoped that the child she was about to bring into the world would make up for the lack she felt that they must endure. She knew that they had wanted their son to have a nice wedding in a church right there in Parkersburg to a girl that they would have known and of whom they would approve. They were thrust into a situation they did not deserve.

"I'm sorry!" she yelled when the pain was getting unbearable. Of course, Mary did not understand what she was sorry about.

When the doctor came back, Florence was about to deliver. At just the right moment, he gave her a whiff of chloroform, and soon the sound of a crying infant was heard.

Mary took care of the little boy. Florence had some pieces of clothing and a few diapers for him. Right away, John said his name should be Butch. Mary wanted it to be Charles Jr., just like his dad, so the doctor went back to the office with the name Charles John Miller and knew little Charles would always be called Butch.

Mary stayed with Florence, even after Chuck came back and left again. She stayed the full ten days as was the custom in those days, and Florence stayed in bed and learned to nurse her baby boy. Mary had to teach her everything about caring for an infant. Florence had not been around a tiny baby before.

Mary washed clothes every day because there were not enough diapers for the little guy for more than two days. After Chuck came home, Mary went shopping for baby clothes for little Charles. She was thrilled with her grandson.

That made it a little easier on Florence when she did get to her feet to take over the job of caring for her family on her own. Washing clothes by hand was a long and time-consuming process.

On the tenth day, Dr. Bruechardt came by and checked Florence out. He told her that she could get up but that she needed to be careful and take it easy.

"Don't overdo it. You had a big baby—over eight pounds. Therefore, I want you to be very careful not to strain yourself. You had a little tearing, and it will take a while to heal."

Dr. Bruechardt delivered babies at home, and they were not weighed on a scale as they are today in hospitals. He had a scale in the office, but he didn't carry one with him. He usually held the baby up and gave an experienced guess. In his estimation, a little over eight pounds was only a guess. He was pretty good at it.

Chuck was walking in the door from his run with the semi and had been at his special café. He said, "Hi, Doc, when can me and the wife have sex?"

Dr. Bruechardt was taken aback. "I can't believe you said that, Chuck. Don't you have any sympathy for your wife? Don't touch her for at least a month. Be careful. Your wife is still bleeding. You haven't even seen your son yet. The little guy looks just like you. You don't know how lucky you are."

Dr. Bruechardt grabbed his bag and left very quickly because he could see Chuck had been drinking and was about to get really nasty.

If Mary had not appeared from the basement, things could have gotten out of hand. She had seen her son when he was drunk many times, and it was never a pretty sight.

"Chuck, I want you to lie down. You need to sleep it off. You are not in any shape right now. I hope you've had something to eat. If not, I will be glad to fix you something."

"Yeah, I ate at Etta's," he responded resolutely.

Mary gave a knowing grunt and let it go. Chuck lay on the couch and was soon snoring.

"Florence, I will get the baby ready for bed, and I want you to lie down. I am staying the night here. Chuck doesn't seem to be himself. Let's all rest now."

Chapter 19

The news got around town fast. Some of the ladies of the town came over and brought little gifts for the baby. One very welcome gift came from Mrs. Dora Warner, who was the wife of the dentist. She lived around the corner and about a half a block east. She didn't often come out about town, but she came because Florence was a newcomer, and Dora felt that Florence needed some company and could use the new diapers for the baby. Dora liked to sew and knew that she could sew diapers from cotton flannel by making only two hems in each diaper. The other sides did not need hemming because the selvage edge was used instead. Also, if you were hemming by hand, it saved quite a lot of time and effort. She also brought a new galvanized bucket to soak the dirty diapers in. It was quite a sight this sophisticated lady walking down the street carrying a bucket full of new diapers that she had just created.

Mary greeted Dora at the door as she approached.

"My goodness, it's Mrs. Warner, Florence," Mary called out.

By this time, Chuck had been long gone again on one of his runs, and it had been ten days since the baby was born.

Dora was a good person. She was especially kind when it came to new babies. She had never had any of her own, and she had always wanted children. She was always there when a new baby came into a family.

She and her husband George had been sweethearts for ten years but had to wait through several significant events before they could wed. For one thing, they wanted to wait for George to finish school first. But just when he was almost finished, his mother became very ill. She needed a great deal of assistance from her son, who had medical training, so he put off finishing his schooling until after his mother passed away.

George built a house in Parkersburg that had an elevator that would take a patient to his office overlooking the roof, and after completing his education and becoming certified, he and Dora finally married. They moved into his fabulous house, but by that time, she could no longer conceive. She was over forty years old by then, and her time was passed.

Dora always hoped that by some miracle, she would conceive. With what she thought was her failure, she took it upon herself to welcome new arrivals, especially on the west side of town. She took a special interest in Florence and her new baby.

Soon Mary sensed that Florence needed to begin to take care of the baby on her own. She had done her best to teach her the basics of childcare, and now Florence really wanted to try to do what was expected. She loved her son and enjoyed being a new mother. Her son was everything to her. She doted on him and took care of his every need. She talked to him and cuddled him and told him how much she loved him even when he couldn't yet understand.

Chuck came home from Etta's one particular evening and heard Florence cooing to her son, and he grabbed Butch from Florence and threatened to bash his head on the concrete, yelling, "If I get rid of him, will that make you love me?"

Paul, who happened to be driving by from his property to the south, skidded the car to a stop and grabbed the baby. "Vut da hell are you doing?" he yelled. "I'm taking dis baby home until you can come to your senses. Are you crazy or vut?"

All the while, little Butchie had been screaming at the top of his lungs. As soon as Paul took him, he quieted down. Chuck had been so taken aback that someone would dare to step in that he stood there dumbfounded. He was actually afraid of Paul, who laid the baby on the car's front seat as he drove home. As he looked out the rearview mirror, he could see Chuck grabbing Florence and dragging her into the house.

91

When Paul got home, he hurriedly grabbed the baby and yelled, "Hey, Minnie, take care of this little guy. I'm going to da town marshal and get him to go over to Florence's. Vee gotta help her out. Chuck is gonna kill dis baby. I'll tell you I'll kill dat son of a bitch before he touches dis baby or Florence ever again."

Off Paul went to the marshal's office. When he told the police officer what he saw and heard, both Paul and Marshal Harry Lumley went to the Miller's home.

As they climbed the front steps, they heard a horrible commotion. There was obviously a huge fight going on. There were sounds of things being smashed, things falling, Florence crying out in pain, Chuck cursing, and a door being slammed. What they heard as they were walking up the steps to the front door and what they saw when entering the house was enough to make Harry arrest Chuck, handcuff him, and take him to the tiny jailhouse by the water tower.

When they went back to the house, Florence was dabbing at her bloody nose and had the beginning of a shiner.

All the time, Paul kept saying, "Dat son of a bitch," over and over. "How da hell can a man treat his vife like dat?"

Harry kept saying, "Now, Paul, calm down, I won't let Chuck out of jail until he calms down, and the judge has a good talking to him."

Paul packed Florence in the car and stopped at Dr. Bruechardt's to have Florence checked out before he took her home to his house. She had a concussion, a broken rib, facial lacerations, along with a black eye and a sprained wrist. Doc stitched her up under the eye and told her to take it easy, put ice on the eye if they could, and sent them on their way. Paul blamed himself for leaving her there with Chuck to take the baby home, but his immediate reaction to the scene he saw was to save the baby. He had wanted a son, and every little boy was a little angel to him.

Minnie had little Butch in her arms as they were coming in the door. "My god, Florence, what happened to you?" Minnie gasped as she came closer to get a better look at Florence's face. By now, her eye was getting more swollen and blacker. She was to lie down and rest because she was woozy from the blow to the head.

Paul went to the pump to get some cold water. They had no refrigerator or even an icebox. Paul decided to go to the Welcome Inn on Main Street and get some ice. It was only a couple of blocks. He was back in less than fifteen minutes.

Florence stayed the night on the small, black leather couch while Minnie and Paul doted over her. The ice seemed to help, but Florence could barely see out of her left eye the next morning. Even though Paul made several trips to the bar to get more ice, it was not like having a bag of ice handy each time the ice melted.

The next morning, Paul took Florence home. He helped her to get the overturned furniture back in place, fixed the hinges on the bedroom door, and made sure that the baby's little bed was secure. He handed Florence the fresh bag of ice they had gotten on the way to Florence's house and left.

Paul stopped at Marshal Lumley's office to see that Chuck was going to stay in jail awhile yet. Since all that was secure, he went on to work.

Chapter 20

After Chuck had some time to cool off in his cell, he began thinking about what had happened. He was furious at Paul for interfering in his private affairs. He did not sleep much. He was cold most of the night. As the sun crept up on the horizon, he began to plan a change in his attitude. He realized that he should be somewhat contrite so that he could get out of there. He could blame everything on the fact that he had been drinking. Maybe if he was nice to the marshal, he could go home and finish what he had started. He dozed off and awoke later in the morning.

When Marshal Lumley came to bring him breakfast from the café downtown, Chuck seemed quite contrite. He apologized for his behavior the previous evening. Marshal Harry Lumley was not in the least convinced by his change in attitude. He knew Chuck was not at all sorry. Harry knew that he just wanted to get out of there and was willing to put on any kind of show to convince Harry to let him go home. Harry was nobody's fool. He was a lawman and had been a good one for a long time.

"I am not convinced that you are really sorry," Harry began. "I think the minute you get out of here, Paul will be back here with you again. You really don't want to be on his bad side. You can't just beat up your wife and son. I tell you that you had better treat your wife with some respect, or you will have the wrath of Paul Adelmund on your hands as well as mine, and I can assure you that you do *not* want that. We will both keep our eyes on you. I am getting the judge here today, and you had better think about what you are going to say. Paul is coming in too. You'd best be thinking about if you really intend to continue the way you are heading or not. Remember that you were caught red-handed. I saw you myself. Worse than that, Paul saw it all. You know that he can be your best friend or your worst enemy. It all depends on you."

As Harry left, he turned on his heel with one more word of advice, "Think. Think about what you have done. If you don't change your ways, there will come a time when you least expect it, that you will wish you had. I'm warning you."

Harry spun back on his heel and left without another word.

That afternoon, the judge came into town from Allison, the county seat. He went to the downtown café on Main Street, had a little lunch, and listened to the talk about the truck driver who beat up his wife. He listened and watched as inconspicuously as possible. When he was finished, he met the marshal in his office behind the jail.

"Well, Harry, what do we have here? I am surprised that you called. You usually don't need me. What do you think I should do? I trust you to handle things. I am surprised that you even called me in."

"Well, I want you to put the fear of God into this guy," Harry replied. "Paul Adelmund saw him trying to kill his own son and beating up on his wife. I really don't want him to experience what Paul and his brothers could do to him. The honor of those guys won't let them stand by and allow him to continue to abuse his wife and possibly kill that little boy. If we catch this problem right away, we won't have any more trouble. What do you think?"

"You've got something there, Harry. I'll sure do what I can. Let's set up court and get the ball rolling," Judge Shepherd replied resolutely. As they walked over to set up the table that served as his bench, Judge Shepherd began by saying, "I full well remember the story about when Paul's brother, John, was in the German Army and accidently killed an officer when he hit him too hard. I remember hearing that since he was in the lower class there, it was automatic that he would go before a firing squad for accidently killing someone of the upper class, even though it was an accident. Because of the officer's elite class and higher rank, John was just supposed to stand there and not raise a fist against him, even though it was the officer who hit him first. As a matter of fact, someone of the lower class could never rise any higher in the army there. Even though there were many witnesses that knew it was an accident and vouched for John, he still would have been put to death. I guess those witnesses were convinced that it would be wrong for him to pay for it with his life. There was absolutely no chance for his survival. From what I hear, Paul broke him out of the stockade and brought him to the US with him. It is said that John was a stowaway on The Reindam, a Dutch ship. When it sprung a leak, Paul got his brother out of hiding, and they manned the pumps and became friends with the captain. It is quite a story. Of course, I'm not sure that I believe it all. On the other hand, we don't want to push the Adelmund boys too far."

After the two men had gone to the small building next to the jail that served as a courtroom and set things up, they began the business at hand. As the marshal went to the jail to pick up the prisoner, Paul showed up. "Hey, Harry, vut are vee gonna do vit dis vife beater and child killer? He woulda killed dat little boy if I vouldn'da stepped in."

Marshal Lumley shook Paul's hand and said, "I don't really know. That's why I got the judge from Allison here, and we'll find out."

The hearing didn't last long. There were several townspeople that wanted to add their two cents' worth, none of which was favorable to Chuck. Many had seen Chuck browbeat and slap his wife and call her names. Minnie came in with Florence, and everyone saw the black and blue and bloodied places on her. She was so sore that she could hardly walk.

The judge was taken aback at the viciousness with which the dirty deed had obviously been inflicted. So swollen were her eyes that she could barely see out of one, whereas the other could not be opened at all.

As the judge questioned her, he had difficulty understanding what she was saying because her lips were so swollen.

Judge Shepherd called a recess so that he could control his anger. He needed to stay calm. As he was standing there drinking a cup of coffee, he visualized that it could be his daughter in there someday if things didn't change. He knew that the laws about how a man treats his wife are lax at best, if not altogether missing. In fact, in 1919, women were finally allowed to cast their votes in general elections. In 1868, the Iowa legislature removed the word "White" from the Iowa constitution to the word "male," making it possible for Black males to vote but not women. Judge Shepherd also knew that many women were still denied the privilege to vote because their husbands would keep them from doing so. Every time the issue came up, "Women are either not smart enough, or they just are not interested in politics and don't know enough about the issues" was always the answer. The judge realized that he could do very little about the situation at hand, so he left for about fifteen minutes to do some checking and think about the case calmly before returning with a decision.

During that time, he made several phone calls and asked several questions of the marshal. He went back in the courtroom and declared, "Chuck, a man like you should be locked up, never to see the light of day again. However, the letter of the law is not clear as to what I should do. If it were anyone other than your wife, I could have you in jail for quite a few years. I am making a decision as judge of Butler County. You will stay in the city jail for a period of two months. Then you will not be allowed to go home. You must stay away from your wife until—or if—she ever says it's okay for you to come back. I don't care where you live, but you will need to live somewhere else until she deems it's all right for you to come home. Meanwhile, your wages will go to Florence through the marshal here. I have investigated your situation at work, and I know that you are still owed for a run you completed prior to this incident, and I have arranged for your check to come to the marshal. He has been given control of your finances while you are under his care. He will make sure that your wife and child will be taken care of while you are cooling your heels here in jail. When you have served your time and go back to work—that is, if you still have a job after two months of being locked up—then the marshal here will still be in control. Each Saturday at 10:00 a.m., you will meet your wife here at the marshal's office, and you will personally hand Florence $25 a week from your paycheck and treat her as she deserves to be treated. You will be able to see your son there, within sight of the marshal. He will teach you how to speak to and treat both of them with love and respect. I hope you'll learn how to treat a woman and child. I am warning you that should you be disrespectful to your wife in any way, you will not only hear from me, but the marshal here, and probably Paul Adelmund as well."

Chuck started to interrupt. The judge stopped him with "You are being warned. If things don't go well during this probation period, I will extend your jail time. Now, Harry, take this scum back to his cell. I just wish we could throw away the key."

Chapter 21

Florence relaxed during the two months Chuck was in jail. She did go to see him, and he always asked her forgiveness. She knew that he was just saying those things within earshot of the marshal so that he could go home when he got out.

Marshal Lumley was not convinced of Chuck's sincerity, but Florence wanted to believe that Chuck would never do anything like that to her again. As long as the bars were between them, Florence felt comfortable visiting Chuck, so she visited him regularly. Marshal Lumley was always there when she came. He also intervened when Chuck's language or mannerisms indicated abusiveness.

Gradually, her physical wounds healed, but there was a nasty scar under her eye and next to her hairline that made her shudder every time she looked in the mirror. It was a constant reminder of that horrible night. One battle over, and she had lost.

"I don't know what to do, Butchie," she said as she cradled her little one. "I sure don't want you to grow up without a dad. I am so afraid that one day he will kill us both. I know that he is jealous of you, sweetheart, because you take up so much of my time and energy. I just don't know what to do. He is getting out soon, and he wants to come home. He needs to go back to work. We are running out of money. He says he'll quit his job, and we won't be able to live if I don't let him come home. It is not easy finding a job these days. I'm also pretty scared about when he does come home. I just don't know what to do, sweetheart. I love you so much."

The next afternoon, Paul, Minnie, and the girls stopped over after working on their new property. It was a slough, and every time

Paul had some leftover dirt from a grave that he had dug, he brought it over and deposited it on the lot on which their new house would be built.

Every day, Paul would come by to see how Florence was getting along. Sometimes, he brought his family along. It would not be long, and Minnie would be delivering another child into their family. The shacks in which they were presently living would be more crowded than ever.

Minnie seemed out of breath when she went up the steps that led to Florence's house. As she looked down, she saw a small stocking near the steps that was thick with mud. When she stopped to bend over and retrieve it, she almost lost her balance. Paul quickly grabbed her. He picked up the sock and shook it.

"Hm," he said, "if I'm not mistaken, dere is dat missing sock dat flew off Butchie venn Chuck shook him dat night. I know he had on only vun sock venn I took him home vit me."

"God, Florence, vut are ya gonna do?" Paul said to her as she welcomed them into her humble home. "I yust vish vee didn't live across town from you. If vee vere closer, I could keep an eye on you better. Try to keep ya safe. None of us have dose newfangled telephones either. I vill come by as often as I can, but I don't know if I can be here enough to make sure nutting happens to you." Changing the subject, he said, "Hey, you're healin' up real good."

Minnie quickly added, "Florence, we worry about you. I'm sure you know that whatever you decide, we will try to be available to help you where, when, and with whatever you need. We mainly came to see how you are doing and to see if you need anything. We'll be going right past Main Street."

"That's really kind of you two, but I have enough to get by on. Chuck's folks have been very kind and understanding. They obviously know their son pretty well and have never been able to control his mean streaks. That is one of the reasons they were so surprised that he brought home a wife. Of course, it wasn't his idea by any stretch of the imagination."

Florence's conversation became mostly about her in-laws, their difficulties with their son, and Chuck's inability to control his temper. She really cared for the Millers. Her mother-in-law was like her own mother to her.

The Millers always were kind people, but since they only had the one son, whom they indulged and coddled, they were always excusing his behavior so that he got by with almost anything. There was only one time that he was punished, and that was when he killed the family dog when he kicked him to death. As Florence continued talking about the Millers in kind and loving ways, it was obvious that she really was attached to them. Even though Chuck told them that it was all Florence's fault that she got beat up, they knew differently, and they told her so.

Now Paul and Minnie knew that Florence had others in her life that might help her when she needed it. This made it a little easier for them not to feel quite as responsible for keeping her safe. Apparently, the Millers stopped by almost every day.

They stayed and had coffee before they left that night. After their conversation with Florence, they went home with a better understanding of what they were dealing with. It was obvious that Chuck's own parents had difficulty taming their son. Any influence they may have had before, they knew now that their son was beyond any positive influence they might still have had.

When they got home that evening, it was rather late, and everyone was really tired, especially Minnie. She was nine months pregnant, and she was having trouble sleeping. The baby was riding high under her ribs, which made her very uncomfortable most of the time, keeping her from sleeping well. Today, it seemed like the baby was riding lower, so maybe she would be able to sleep tonight.

Minnie awoke with a start the next morning and realized that she was in labor. She woke Paul and told him that he should get the doctor.

When Dr. Bruechardt arrived, he looked Minnie over well and told her that she would be in labor most of the day and not to worry. As he left, he said, "Well, Minnie, you've been down this road before, so you know how it goes. I'll check on you about noon. I hope you'll have someone come in and help today."

"Yeah. I'll get Becky Allison, who lives right next door. She has helped me before," Minnie related.

"Oh yes, I remember the last time when Wilma was born three years ago that Becky helped. Actually, I'll go over and ask her myself," Doc replied. When the doctor left, Paul stayed with Minnie until Becky arrived, which to him seemed like a long time.

It was early in the morning, and Becky had to get dressed for the day and comb her hair. She knew that it could take quite a while, but she also knew that each time is very different. The last time the baby came early and was barely five pounds. The little thing couldn't even nurse. Minnie's milk dried up, and the baby was given oatmeal water. Oatmeal was boiled briefly, the water poured off, and a little sugar was added. And she thrived until she was able to eat some solids. She was covered all over with black hair when she was born, and she still had hair on her back, legs, arms, and lots of thick black hair on her head. That was quite a sight. Minnie always called her a throwback to the apes.

She was not kind in regard to that little girl, Becky thought as she hurried over to Minnie's. Now the little girl was almost three and was filling out a little, so Becky thought that maybe Minnie would let up on her a little.

She thought about these things as she walked. She also thought about last year when Minnie was helping to wallpaper the upstairs in her mother-in-law's, Alice's, house. Little Wilma supposedly fell down the stairs, but Minnie saw Alice push her. Minnie knew she resented Wilma, simply because she had wanted her to be named Jacobine Wilhelmine. Minnie wouldn't give a child such a handle; so as a compromise and in keeping with their Dutch heritage, Minnie decided to shorten the child's name to Wilma Jean, after the queen of Holland, in the hopes that this would make Alice happy and still sound similar to the name she had suggested. Unfortunately, this wasn't good enough for Alice, and she took it out on poor little Wilma. Becky had seen Minnie as she walked by her house later that day, dragging Pauline and Wilma with her from Alice's. Minnie was trying to comfort her little one and stopped her from crying while also berating her for following her upstairs. But Wilma knew that her grandmother didn't like her, so she had wanted to stay upstairs by her mom. After this incident, Minnie never left Wilma alone with her grandmother again.

When Becky arrived, she became quite concerned because there was something different about the situation. It seemed Minnie seemed quite different than she had been before, during her last two deliveries. She seemed somewhat apprehensive. She heard Minnie ask Paul if he would go to Waterloo and bring back her mother, Lena. Paul thought that was odd, but he readily agreed to go. It was summer, and he felt that he could get there and back before dark. It was June 4, 1939. The last time Minnie gave birth, it was August 1936, which had been a horribly hot year. This was pleasant weather.

Speaking Platt, the Low German, as was the usual way that Paul and Minnie spoke to each other, he said, "I'll leave right away. I'm sure Lena will come gladly. Be careful and rest until I get back. Becky is here now, so I will go and be back as soon as I can." At that, Paul bent down, kissed his wife, and went out the door.

As he drove off in his old '29 Chevy, he knew that he would be wondering about what was happening at home the whole time. Paul always carried on a conversation full voice with himself.

"I sure hope dis is going to be a boy. If it is, I vill sing to him and put him to bed every night. I sure do vunt a boy. Vee vill name him Vernon after his Aunt Verna. I vunt to name my boy a regular American name, not vut my mom vunts. In dis country, vee should have American names. I don't vunt a Jakobus, I vunt a Vernon Eugene. I'll call him Vern. Yeah, I vunt a boy. Hell, maybe I can't make any boys."

He laughed out loud. He could always entertain himself—after all, he was his own best audience. Paul started to sing his German lullaby for his son. Translated, the first line of the song would be "Sleep now, my little son, my beloved are you." Paul sang it all the way to Lena's house in Waterloo.

At 520 Oneida, he knocked on the door, and Minnie's sister Pauline came to the door.

"Hi, Paul, what is the matter? You look worried" came the question at the door.

"Hi, I need to talk to Lena. Minnie is going to have our baby today, and she vunts her mom to be dere."

Pauline opened the door wider as she led Paul into the kitchen, where Lena was cooking one of her favorite dishes of kale. Kale was growing well in her garden to the side of the house. They had two lots. The lot on which the house stood was facing Oneida. The corner lot was at the intersection of Oneida and Mobile. There the garden was placed, surrounded by a hedge and three fruit trees. Although the soil was somewhat sandy, Fred Spars kept it clean of weeds, and his experience made things grow well. Lena also knew a great deal about gardening. Everything she touched always grew well and produced bountifully.

Lena was in the kitchen, peeling potatoes. She could peel them so thin that the peel would come off in one continuous curled piece.

"Hi, Paul, come on in and sit down." Fred Spars appeared from the porch and shook Paul's hand as he spoke.

"I really can't, Fred. I came to get Lena. I hope you vill take care of tings here. I need to get home. Minnie is going to have our baby any time now, and she vunts her mom." Of course, much of this conversation was a mixture of Low German and English.

Immediately, Lena said, "I'll be right there." She gathered a few things and was out the door in less than ten minutes. Before leaving, she shouted up the stairs, "Hey, Verna, you girls take care of everything. I have dinner going now, but I have to go to Minnie. She needs me. I don't know how long I'll need to be gone. You just never know about these things. Take care of things here for me. Bye for now!"

Verna yelled back, "Don't worry, Ma, I'll get everything ready before I go to work. Give Minnie my best!"

"I will!" yelled Lena.

Verna was a seamstress at Powers, a manufacturing plant that produced sportswear for schools. She had the three to eleven shift. She would ride the city buses to and from work. This was a really good system, except for the four-block walk before and after the ride. Fred Spars usually would get up at night to meet Verna's bus after her shift at 11:00 p.m. He was a kind and good man. Minnie, however, never said anything good about him because she felt betrayed that her mother married him after her first husband's death. Minnie was too young to realize that her mother had to find a way to survive. Lena appreciated Fred Spars, and although she was not in love with him the way she was with Paul Viel, she needed someone to help her raise her children. She had no way of supporting herself and her children.

Paul and Lena got in the car and were finally on their way to Parkersburg. Lena kept asking questions about the situation at home. Their conversation was easygoing because Paul respected Lena and really liked her. Lena was only a few years older than Paul, and she had also immigrated from the old country. They talked about the happenings in Europe. Austria had been taken over by Hitler's army earlier, along with other territories that had been part of Germany before WWI.

"God, I'm glad I am not dere now," Paul said. "I fear for my two sisters and dere families in Ostfriesland. If dis country gets involved, I could have some of my sister's kids shooting some of my brudder's kids from here or dee utter vay around."

Lena was fearful for family members that she still had in Holland. Although she would lose family to the Germans, she had no way of knowing that in June of 1939. In fact, one of her cousins there married a kind and gentle man who happened to be Jewish. When Holland was taken over by Germany later in the war, her cousin's husband was slaughtered right before her eyes. At this time, Lena was, of course, oblivious to what the future would hold for her generation.

Little did her son-in-law know at the time that his words would prove true later in the war. Paul's sister, Angel, was later killed by allied bombing, and her husband—who was also the brother-in-law of Paul's brother Abbo—was in the German Army. He was killed in France. This affected all the Adelmunds in America. A number of the Adelmund boys—sons of Paul's brothers—did serve valiantly in the American armed forces during WWII. Bill Junior was actually in the Army infantry in Germany. There was a relative, who was a tail gunner in a B17 over Germany when Tante Angel's house was bombed, and she was killed. No one knows if that was the same B17 as the one that killed Angel. As the story goes, the B17 was dropping its bombs to lighten the load because it had been crippled by ack-ack fire and was headed back to England. Ostfriesland, the Adelmund homeland in Germany, is right on the coast of the North Sea with England on the other side of it.

Two of Abbo's boys were in the American Navy. All of Paul's brothers' children were older than Paul and Minnie's. They married earlier in life than Paul did, so many of them were of draft age before and during the war. Some enlisted before the United States actually declared war in December of 1941. Of course, many of Lena's family also served for the United States in WWII.

Chapter 22

*P*aul and Lena arrived in Parkersburg around noon. Becky met them outside. She told Paul that she thought the doctor should get there soon. They went in, and Minnie was sweating. It was obvious that she was in hard labor.

Becky grabbed both little girls and took them to her house. They were both crying because they were concerned for their mom. They knew she was in pain. "Now, now, girls, I have some cookies I made just yesterday. Don't worry about your mom. She'll be okay. There will soon be a new baby in your house."

Paul was heading for the Chevy Garage to go to work as Dr. Bruechardt pulled up. "Glad to see you, Doc. Minnie could use some help."

"That's what I'm here for" came the answer. They both went into the house.

Dr. Bruechardt told him, "Paul, this may only take a little while. Now don't go off to work. Why don't you go over to your brother's house across the street and have some coffee? Lena and I can take care of this. I think Minnie would like you nearby, so don't go far."

As Paul left, he yelled, "Give me a boy this time, Doc."

"I have nothing to do with that part, Paul. That is your doing," Doc laughed.

As he headed across the street, Abbo's two girls met him. Angeline and Leona greeted him with smiles and a hug. "What's going on, Uncle Paul?"

"Hi, girls, I'd like to see your dad and mom. Does Lena [Abbo's wife's name was also Lena] have the coffee pot on? I could sure use a cup. Minnie's in labor, and I don't really vunt to be dere. I can't stand seeing her in pain. Duh kids are at Becky's house, and I told my boss dat it could be dat I'd not be dere today because of duh baby coming. I vunt to have a boy so bad."

At that, Abbo greeted them at the door, "Well, Paul, we live so close, but you are always so busy that we don't get to see you often enough. I'll get my accordion, and we'll sing."

"That sounds like a hellava good idea. Minnie is having our baby as we speak, and vee can celebrate!" Paul fairly shouted with glee.

There sure was music in those Adelmund boys. They all could play and sing with harmony and definitely knew how to have a good time.

When Paul drank his coffee, first saucering it and blowing it so he could drink it fast, he sighed. "Ya venn you poos it, it cools it off qvick, dat makes a difference." He directed his remark to Leona, who was looking at him quizzically.

"Uncle Paul, you talk just like my dad. I guess you'll never lose your accent either," Leona remarked and added, "I just never really noticed it so much before. Yeah, you need to poos it. After all, it is boiling hot."

Abbo chimed in with "Ya mine, brudder, he does better mit da langvitch denn I do, I tink." Everyone laughed at that.

Abbo reached in the closet and retrieved his button accordion. They all began to sing the old German folk songs, as they often did, such as "Du, Du Liegst Mir Im Herzen" and "Die Lorelei." Paul's favorite was always "Hav Vee Noch 'N Drupke." Sometimes they would also sing American folk songs, such as "Oh, Susanna" and "You Are My Sunshine."

Paul began singing his lullaby for a son. When he finished, his eyes were filled with tears. He did want a son so badly. Although the Adelmund boys were tough, their emotions were displayed easily. The tears usually came when they sang songs of Germany and when they thought of the many wars and deaths that were experienced there. They thought of their brother Jacobus (Jake) when he was struck down in WWI. Paul always said that when he and Jake would walk down the street in town with their arms wide open, Jake would always get two girls to fill his arms, and he would only get one. The lost brother was always part of the equation in their minds. He was always the handsomest one, the toughest one, and the one not with them. There always seemed to be a war going on in Germany. Its borders changed so very many times in its history.

The coffee pot was empty when Lena knocked on the door and said, "Paul, you have a boy! You have your little Vernon Eugene! He is healthy and about seven and a half pounds. Everything is fine, and the doctor is just leaving. You will need to take care of the afterbirth. The doctor said that you would know what to do."

Paul raced across the street and was way ahead of Lena and burst in the door as he yelled, "A boy! Vee did it, Minnie! Vee have a boy." He hugged Minnie and took the baby in his arms and began to sing, "Schlaff nun mein Sönchen, mein Liebling bis' Du."

Soon Abbo was at the door and brought a schnapps, and the two brothers had a drink together in celebration of the great day. This was a day of the birth of a son! Although there were fourteen children in the original Adelmund family, there had been only two girls. The second generation was the total opposite. There were only a few boys but lots of girls.

Becky brought the two girls over after Abbo left, and soon all was quiet in the shacks except for the beautiful tenor voice of Paul singing his lovely lullaby to his son as he gently rocked Vern, all the while beaming in sheer and glorious ecstasy saying over and over, "I can't believe it. I have a son in my arms." Everyone else was resting. Only Lena was awake and keeping an eye on Paul and the baby, just to make sure that Paul would not fall asleep with the child in his arms. Finally, Lena said, "I think Vern has been asleep for the last hour. If you want to go to work tomorrow, you will need your rest."

Paul handed Vern to Lena and said, "Ya, it is late, and I am tired. Thanks, Lena. Good night." He, too, was soon snoring, and he was good at that. It was a blessed day for everyone.

Chapter 23

After the usual ten day's bed rest, Dr. Bruechardt came over to Paul and Minnie's. Minnie was now allowed to get up but was supposed to take it somewhat easy. Lena was still there and insisted that she would get all the laundry done and the house cleaned before she would go home. This, of course, would take the entire day since the laundry was done on a washboard and wrung out by hand. Because the weather was so lovely, she would hang the clothes outside on the clotheslines with clothespins until they were dry. It was a Friday, and Paul would be at work. Then on Sunday, he would take her back to Waterloo. It was a beautiful day, and Minnie decided to take the girls for a walk across the tracks to the Beaver Creek. That way, they would be out of the way so Lena could get some work done.

Minnie liked to listen to the water and watch the ducks and geese. Her mind flew back to the times she used to swim across the Cedar River in Waterloo. She was an excellent swimmer and loved to do the butterfly stroke.

Lena was very happy to take care of the little boy. The only problem was that Pauline also wanted to stay home with her grandmother because she thought she could talk Lena into baking some cookies for her like Becky Allison did. At her mother's insistence, Minnie decided to take just Wilma. She held the little girl's hand, and they walked slowly, just enjoying the flowers, the sound of the creek, and being together. Minnie spotted a swing in a weeping willow tree, and she gently pushed her little daughter in the swing as they laughed together. It was the first time the two of them had some time together, just the two of them. It would be one of the fondest memories Wilma would have of her mother—so much so, that many decades later, she even wrote a song about it. She adored her mother and would do everything her mother asked her to do even when the chores she did were really too hard for her, especially when she was asked to carry things or lift things much too heavy for her small size and weight.

Wilma was thrilled to be able to have her mom all to herself. This had never happened before. She was giddy with excitement and anticipation. This was something she had always dreamed about, and it was just as she thought it would be. That one-half hour would be embedded in her brain for the rest of her life. This time, it was not work that she was doing. It was just pure joy to be alone with her mom, especially with her mom happy and content.

When they arrived back at the shacks, Pauline met them outside, pouting. She complained, "Grandma didn't make no cookies for me." When she found out about the swing, she really got upset. She had also missed out on the pleasure of going to the creek. She was not at all happy. She couldn't imagine that grandma wouldn't cave in to her demands. Grandma also had her doing some dusting, which she hated. Minnie never made cookies. The family was lucky to get three meals a day as it was. Minnie told her, "Pauline, if I'd have known that you thought Grandma would bake you cookies, I would have insisted that you come with us. But since you were selfish, you got what you deserved—nothing. I don't feel sorry for you at all."

Pauline never forgot that lesson, but she always held it against Wilma.

All of a sudden, Lena yelled from indoors. As it turned out, it had been a long time since she had remembered how to change a diaper on a boy, and she had gotten "nailed" as soon as the cool air hit Vern's little bottom. The last ten days, she somehow had been lucky, and it hadn't happened. She washed her face with gusto, all the while laughing that she'd forgotten the little trick of placing a towel over the genitals of a little boy when the diaper was changed to avoid the inevitable pee shower.

When the time neared that Lena had to go home, Minnie knew that it was going to be quite a busy summer. There was the garden, and as things matured, they needed to be "put up" to provide food for the winter. This was labor-intensive work. With three children, canning, trying to keep the shacks somewhat cleaned, and cooking, Minnie was really hard put for any downtime. Florence would come over with Butch and help several times each week, and this was a welcome respite for Minnie. They worked together well. The girls also pitched in to help as much as they could. They helped take care of the two little boys and kept Butchie and Vern entertained by singing to them. They even made up games to play because they had no toys to speak of that they could have used to keep the boys' attention.

The best part of it all was that Minnie and Florence's friendship became the bright spot in Florence's life. She enjoyed being around all the children. She had always wanted a big family, and she relished having a part in Minnie's children's lives. She longed for another child of her own and hoped that if things would stabilize with Chuck, she would maybe have several more. That was her dream.

The two little boys soon recognized each other. Vern sometimes became confused about the name "Butch" however. When the family would visit in Waterloo at his grandma's house, his aunt Verna always called Vern "Butch." That was her special name for him. His aunt Verna adored him. He finally got it all figured out when he was about three years old. He knew if he was at Grandma's, he would answer to any of his three names: Vern, Butch, or Butchie.

Lena was a wonderfully patient, kind grandmother. Minnie's children were the only grandchildren she had at the time. They were within 30 miles of her. (At the time, Waterloo was still about an hour drive from Parkersburg.) Now she really got to know her grandchildren quite well. They could celebrate the holidays together and help each other when the need arose. Thanksgiving was usually spent together if the weather held. Every time she saw the family, she talked about when she came for Vern's birth, and, of course, she always mentioned the time she got nailed while changing Vern's diaper. She really did everything she could to make all the children feel welcome when they came to see her several Sundays a year. Those Sundays, she made a big meal and made sure special things, like celery or Jell-O, were served on those occasions. These were things that couldn't come out of Paul and Minnie's garden. The children were not accustomed to such fancy foods. There was very little money to spend on such things. Lena always went out of her way to make sure that everyone left well-fed, and she wanted to expose the children to a little more sophisticated way of life.

Transportation was always an issue. Cars were never reliable. Keeping them running and tires inflated was a real challenge. Gas was cheap. You could buy five gallons for a dollar. However, when the war was in full swing, you needed to have rationing stamps to buy gasoline. Those little books of stamps were more valuable than money. You needed them to buy sugar, liquor, tires, and many other things that were scarce, such as coffee. That way, people didn't waste anything.

The children liked going to their grandma's house. They were especially intrigued by the real live toilet upstairs in her house! They couldn't believe that you could actually go potty in the house, and it wasn't the white bucket with the lid that was used at night in emergencies or when you were sick. You also had that nice white paper to use instead of catalogs or newspapers. In the outhouse, if you wanted the makeshift toilet paper to be softer, you used the sitting time to the fullest because the whole time you sat there, you had to crunch up the paper to make it a little less harsh. It was still never comfortable no matter how much you scrunched it up. Nothing you did could make it soft like the nice white paper in Grandma's bathroom.

The outhouse was never a pleasant place to be. It smelled bad. There were spiders and hornets and all kinds of unpleasant things in there. It was especially bad in the cold Iowa winters. It was scary at night and was even worse when you had to fight the cold of winter too.

Living during the 30s and 40s was hard enough, but with the rumors of war on the horizon, it became even worse. Even if you had money during the war, you still couldn't buy what you needed because everything was devoted to the men and matériel needed to make war. So many things were impossible to get, and many things you really needed you couldn't buy if you didn't have the correct rationing stamps. And talk about recycling! Everything was saved. If you had a stick of gum, the foil was meticulously pulled from the paper and saved in balls. The string that wrapped your meat or cheeses at the grocery store was also tied together and made into huge balls that were used for the war effort. The aluminum foil was used to confuse the enemy's radar so our soldiers would not be spotted by them. It was a period of intense pulling together. Everyone did whatever they could to help win the war. In school, everyone stood for morning prayer, seeking God's help for the end of the war, and that the soldiers would be able to come home. The pledge of allegiance was recited every morning as well; however, the phrase "under God" was not yet part of it at that time. That came about during Eisenhower's administration in the 50s. Everyone was tuned into the radio to hear Franklin Roosevelt's fireside speeches. And each day, everyone waited in their towns and villages to find out if their boys were still alive. Usually, the mail brought the news. Few people actually had telephones. Those were only for the rich.

This was the situation during the Second World War period of history in the small towns of the United States of America.

Chapter 24

As 1939 wore on, Germany invaded Poland in September. The world watched as Hitler became evermore greedy. He appeared to be invincible as he grabbed country after country. Britain seemed to be the only country that was trying to stop him.

There were rumors that certain groups of people were disappearing, and no one seemed to be certain of where they had gone. America did not want to get involved in this war, and American isolationists were pushing to stay out of the conflict. World War I was still very vivid in everyone's minds. There were millions of Americans that were of German descent who couldn't believe that the German people had actually elected Hitler. How could they elect someone that was so insane? However, it didn't seem so at the beginning when he first took office in 1933, and German Americans didn't fully understand that the depression that had taken place in America was worldwide, and as a result, people everywhere were starving. When someone promises prosperity and is told, "Everyone will have 'a chicken in every pot' and 'a car in every garage,'" it is simply human nature to follow that path, even more so when you are hungry.

The Nazis were very much aware of the fact that if a lie is told over and over enough times, people will begin to believe it, and they tend to believe that if there is smoke, there is fire, even if the smoke turns out to be water vapor. People believe lies all the time. Just think of the time when some people actually believed that President Obama wasn't a natural-born American citizen. That lie was perpetrated by Donald Trump even though he knew it was a lie, but somehow people believed him anyway, simply because they wanted to. No matter how many times President Obama's birth certificate had been produced, people still believed the lie. People believe what they want to believe even when there is valid proof to the contrary. Even with eyes to see and ears to hear, what they want to believe, they will, and that is a proven fact. Unfortunately, almost anyone can be led astray by statements that are presented as valid when they are actually unfounded, especially when those statements are made by respected people. Even Colin Powell was hoodwinked into believing there were weapons of mass destruction in Iraq, causing the invasion after 9/11 during George W. Bush's presidency. They never existed. False documentation was created. Of course, if the president of the United States says something is a fact, we are prone to believe it, even if the documentation presented to back it up turns out to be false. After all, we don't want to believe we are wrong or that a president would actually lie to us. There seemed to be a "we want revenge even if we are wrong, and somebody has to pay" attitude after that tragic day of 9/11. Although there may have been a feeling of relief that something was being accomplished, it certainly did nothing for our security and lowered the United States' esteem in the eyes of the world at large.

Minnie, meanwhile, tried hard to keep Paul from worrying so much about his family in Germany, though she had said repeatedly that she wouldn't want any son of hers to be cannon fodder, especially if Paul's relatives were the ones doing the shooting. The whole thing really hit home when her brother Ray enlisted in the Navy in 1939. Sometime later, her friends, the five Sullivan brothers, enlisted in the Navy as well. They enlisted with the stipulation that they be kept together so that they could take care of each other.

Minnie was worried about all of them. She had bad dreams about her brother and her close friends. Many were the times when she couldn't think of anything else but the war, even though she tried very hard not to dwell on world affairs. Everyone was saying that with America sandwiched between two oceans, there was no need to worry about anything. Little did America know that there was also trouble brewing in the Pacific. Japan, in cahoots with Germany, was taking over China and many islands in the Pacific Ocean.

Army General Billy Mitchell had told the US Congress about the nationalism that was rising in Japan and warned the United States to be ready for trouble. However, the powers that be in America did not believe him, and, consequently, the US was not prepared for the attack on Pearl Harbor. At the very same time, the attack was taking place, Japanese envoys in Washington, DC, were promising peace. This was simply a diversion to make sure that the attack was never suspected—a ruse to catch America off guard. The Pearl Harbor surprise attack was Yamamoto's plan to immobilize the United States before war was ever declared.

It had been a beautiful Sunday morning on December 7, 1941, on the island of Oahu, Hawaii, when suddenly all hell broke loose at Pearl Harbor. The bombing was horrific. Ships were exploding, and there was utter chaos. People were screaming and running. Fire was everywhere.

Minnie's brother Ray was at Pearl Harbor on that fateful day. He suffered a broken leg on the slippery deck and was badly burned when he was thrown into the sea as his ship went down. The water was on fire because of the burning fuel and oil from the sunken ships. Ray just barely survived.

The Army Air Force also had an airfield nearby, and it was turned to rubble, along with planes, pilots, and hangars. A few planes were able to get off the ground when they began to realize that this was an actual act of war against the United States by the Japanese who were pretending to be friends. The world would never be the same again. Total casualties: 2,403 killed—109 marines, 218 army soldiers, 2,008 sailors, 68 civilians. The sunken *Arizona* battleship alone took with it 1,177 sailors.

That very day—December 7, 1941, "a day that will live in infamy," as President Roosevelt stated—the United States declared war on both Germany and Japan, even though America was definitely not prepared for any conflict. At the time, the United States was helping England and France with the lend-lease program, which was a way of providing war matériel to them. Young men and women began enlisting in the armed services, not only in the US, but also many had already gone to Canada and England to sign up. This was especially true of flyers.

Germany was allied with Italy and Russia also during this period. It was only when Germany invaded Russia in an operation called "Barbarossa" that Russia was forced to change sides and became an "ally" with Britain, America, France, and China.

Paul and Minnie continued working on their new property. Minnie would walk there with the children in tow and stop by Florence's every so often. By this time, it seemed that Chuck was treating her better. The mandatory payments that Florence received for household expenses made it easier for her to take care of the baby. She didn't seem to care—or maybe she didn't even know—that Etta was always there to "comfort" Chuck and feed him at her restaurant. Women just always seemed to see him as needy and would try to fulfill his every desire. They would be blinded to his irresponsible and selfish persona. They were oblivious to his mean streak and his obsession with always needing to be the biggest fish in the fishbowl. His constant need for attention was easy for his women to fulfill, particularly if they would see him only occasionally and for short periods of time. Such behavior would soon become tiresome and difficult on a daily basis. Since his runs across the country would only allow him short visits, he was always welcomed with open arms.

Some days, Becky Allison would take care of Minnie's children when she walked over to the new place to do some work. Minnie staked out where she wanted the house and did other jobs on the property. She was working hard, leveling some of the fill dirt. On her way home one day in September, she decided to stop to have a cup of tea with Florence. She was wondering how Florence was doing, and the two of them chatted for a short while. She was there for about twenty minutes and suddenly realized that supper needed to be started very soon, so she left abruptly.

As she was nearing home, she heard one of her children crying. She hurried home and found Becky with a sobbing Wilma in her arms. The little girl had crawled up on the roof of the porch to get away from Pauline, who was picking on her. Becky had gone out to check on the girls just as Wilma had fallen on some large rocks below. Minnie arrived shortly after, and when Wilma saw her mom, she stopped crying. Since she seemed fine at that point, no one suspected anything was amiss. She did, however, favor her arm for some time after that, but it wasn't until six weeks later when Minnie was bathing her daughter that she noticed a lump that had developed on the right shoulder. When Minnie took her to the doctor, he discovered that her collarbone had been broken in that fall and needed to be broken anew and reset. The doctor taped the arm to her body. It stayed like that until it healed. Several months later, when the six-inch-wide tape was removed with quick jerks, the hair and some skin came with it. Wilma thought, *Well, at least I don't have all that hair on my back anymore.* She was only three years old. The hair never came back.

In October of 1939, Abbo's son, Hank Adelmund, and his family had needed a place to live. Since Paul and Minnie's lot across from Abbo's was rather large, they decided that Hank could move a trailer house close to the edge of the lot to the east. He was offered the opportunity to buy the lot if he wanted to when Paul and Minnie moved to the new place. This would also give Paul and Minnie a little extra money to begin construction. He agreed to it, and soon they helped Hank and Sophie to get settled in. They shared their well and outhouse and were also welcomed to use the cave for storage. Their son Ronnie was about the same age as Wilma, and the two of them got along very well. Ronnie had trouble seeing, so Wilma tried to help him stay safe. He didn't know where the yard ended and the road began, so it was a good thing that he had his cousin to help him. The doctors couldn't agree on what the problem was, but when Ronnie was older, he always wore thick eyeglasses.

Hank and Sophie liked living on that lot. They thrived and had several children there. None of the rest of the children had the difficulty with their eyes like Ronnie did. It was similar to the difference between Paul and Minnie's two children. Pauline had trouble with her eyes, and Wilma never did. Minnie often wondered if there was some reason linked with the lot or the water but never mentioned it to anybody. Why was it the firstborn? she wondered.

As late fall and winter came, work on the new place and all other outside work came to a halt. The problem of staying warm became the biggest priority, and much work needed to be done just to keep warm in the shacks. Firewood needed to be gathered, cut, split, and hauled in. It was always messy with the bark falling off, and it was wet with snow as it was brought in to be used. There was a constant mess from it, and the family was always trying to keep the mess to a minimum as much as possible.

The shacks were not a very cozy home. In the winter, where the two separate shacks were pulled together to form a single dwelling, snowdrifts would form. One needed to wear boots inside the house—not only to keep warm but also to keep the feet dry while sweeping the snow out after it had sifted in. The water pail froze solid during the night. In the morning, a fire was started in the cookstove in the kitchen and in the heating stove in the dining/living area so the ice in the pail would melt. The coffee pot was also filled with water and the coffee added in the evening so that when the kitchen stove was fired up in the morning, it would melt the water and begin the process of making coffee. Such was the life of many people in the small towns and the country during that era in the Midwest. This was the winter of 1939–1940, which was at least milder compared to past winters—especially the winter of 1936, when temperatures plummeted to a record-breaking 33 degrees below zero.

Life itself was always a challenge no matter who you were but most especially for those who had to piece together what would be a meager income at best. Just living was a constant struggle.

Chapter 25

As winter subsided and the spring finally came, it was decided that Paul and Minnie could begin to work on the basement of the new house. Digging the basement by hand would take a long time. One day, Paul's brothers, Harm, Nann, and Abbo, came over to see the new lot across the street from Oak Hill Cemetery. Minnie happened to be there when they offered to help dig. In the end, it became mostly Minnie and Harm, who would actually get the job done. The digging went on for most of the summer and fall.

During that spring of 1940, Minnie and Florence became the closest of friends. The garden was planted, and Minnie was at the new property constantly. She continued digging the basement. The spring rains and the winter had done quite a bit of damage, especially since the lot consisted mostly of fill dirt, and the one side had caved in. Minnie was quite discouraged, as much of the work done before had to be done all over again. However, she tried to hide her despair and bravely continued digging. The neighbor two doors down the street happened to be her aunt Olive Williams, who was married to her mom's, Lena's brother. She was kind enough to come over with her little adopted son, Billy, to help keep the children occupied just as Minnie was about to give up in frustration.

"Hi, Minnie, how's the basement coming?" Olive called as she walked up. Ollie was truly a good person and such a devoted wife and mother. She was always congenial and happy. She and her husband Heiko never fought, and they always respected each other. Heiko was a hard worker. He was the custodian of Oak Hill Cemetery, where every grave was mowed, trimmed, and each stone was cemented with a perpetual cane plaque embedded in it. He was the sole person who did all that work. The only time he had any help was when Paul dug a grave and filled it back in after the casket was lowered. He knew where to dispose of the extra soil that was left over. Heiko then seeded or replaced the sod. He shoveled the roads when there was a funeral in the winter so that the cars and hearse could get through, and he did everything in his power to keep the cemetery beautiful. He was well respected and never complained. He was a good man.

"Not so good, Ollie, I could use a break," Minnie replied. "I'm redoing some of what I did last fall. The spring rains want to take over this land once again, and I am not gonna let it, I'll tell you that. Sometimes, I feel like I bit off more than I can chew, and sometimes, I get discouraged. Why is life such a struggle?"

"I don't know, Minnie, but come on over. I have the teakettle on. I'll help you with the kids." Ollie put her son in the buggy alongside Vern and pushed it over to her house, which was one lot away from Paul and Minnie's land. Aunt Olive had some cookies and Kool-Aid, nice and cold. The kids seemed to like having a break too.

Heiko was there for tea every day when he took a break from his work across the street. Olive always had lunch ready for him at noon and tea at 3:00 p.m. Although he was close to home and it would be easy to laze around home much of the time, he was dedicated to his job and took pride in his beautiful cemetery.

After a little respite and a couple of cups of tea, Minnie headed back to her job on the lot. As she dug, the girls helped by taking the dirt and filling in the holes and indentations that had been left as the fill dirt settled during the spring rains and the winter snows. The baby buggy was there with little Vernon in it. When necessary, Minnie would stop to nurse him.

As the days wore on, Minnie's brother-in-law Harm would come every so often to help dig. The entire summer of 1940 was used for digging the basement—by hand, of course. When Paul would get home from work, he would dig also. He was an expert with a spade. Soon a ladder was needed to get in and out of the hole. Paul's brother

Nann brought his homemade ladder, which served the purpose just fine. Once in a while, he would grab a spade and dig a little too.

Paul also dug a tile ditch that went from the center of the basement floor to the deep ditch along the street to the south. He placed tiles in the ditch and covered them with dirt, thereby averting the problem of water in the basement from the start.

Of course, at the shacks, the garden was also in need of work throughout that time. Potatoes and carrots would be dug up and put in the "cave," as Paul called it, for the coming winter. Not everyone had a cave. As a professional digger, Paul came up with the idea of digging his own underground shelter where they could keep food year-round. This functioned as a sort of natural underground refrigeration system. It was sometimes also called a "storm cellar," where the family could go if a tornado came.

When you looked at the cave from the shacks, all you could see was an eight-foot by ten-foot mound of dirt about 3 feet high in the approximate shape of an elongated oval that was covered with grass. As you looked from the very front, first, you would see a door leaning backward at about a 45-degree slant. When the door was opened, you could see steps going down into the darkness. Once your eyes adjusted to the dark, you could see quite well as long as the door stayed open. Paul had a kerosene lamp hanging on the post to the left that you could light if it was later in the evening and too dark to see. The cave was fitted with special bins made out of planks for storing potatoes, carrots, and cabbage. There were also some shelves on which fruit jars were placed. Other vegetables such as tomatoes, green beans, and peas, plus fruit from the apple tree, were canned and placed under the bed. Sometimes, those would freeze in the winter and could be heard breaking—which could be unnerving, considering they were stored in the old dynamite boxes that were kept under the bed! Those boxes were plentiful because of Paul's work building roads with the construction company as the dynamite expert. They were very sturdy and were also used for many other things. They were even set on end for use as tables.

Early that fall, Pauline started school in kindergarten. Although it was only three afternoons per week, it was still an adjustment for the family. The school was only three blocks away up the hill to the west and south. Soon Pauline was walking to school with her cousins who were in high school, all in the same building. Her cousin Angeline was especially good with her.

One day on a Saturday in September, Pauline decided to take Wilma to school to play on the swings. Minnie was busy cleaning the house, which was done once per week, every Saturday. She didn't notice that the girls were missing, but they could easily be found playing with the Stickley children across the street or at Abbo and Lena's talking with their girls and listening to Abbo playing the accordion or even at Becky's. It was a nice day, so after Minnie finished cleaning, she wanted to bathe the girls outside under the apple tree in the laundry tub. The water had been sitting in the sun since morning, and it was nice and warm now.

Minnie went outside and called for the girls. Vern was sleeping, and she really wanted to get the baths done before the sun went down.

"Pauline Alice, Wilma Jean," she called. No response. She yelled some more. No response. She gave a shrill whistle. No response. She went to the neighbors. No one had seen the girls. The entire neighborhood went searching. Angeline came home from her weekend job and said that she had seen the girls and that they had said they were going to play on the swings at school.

"Pauline said that you had told her they could go," Angeline offered. "The strangest thing, I walked up there to take them home, and they weren't there. I thought that they had come home on their own. I'm sorry, but I didn't notice them anywhere along the way."

Minnie started up the sidewalk toward the west. Instead of turning south up the next street and coming up behind the school, which was the easiest route, she went to the business district, which also would go directly to the school but wind up in front of the school when she turned south. She went all the way to the school but didn't see the girls.

Meanwhile, after spending an hour on the swings, the slide, the monkey bars, and merry-go-round, Wilma wanted to go home. Pauline had pushed her round and round, and Wilma was not feeling well. Pauline finally let her off when she got sick to her stomach. They headed for home, but on the way, she wanted to stop by the old hotel that was on the corner across from the train station. Pauline knew that the latticework was loose under the boardwalk on the side of the building. She took Wilma in under the steps. When Minnie had gone by, Pauline told Wilma that she had to be quiet because that was part of a game. After Minnie was gone, the girls slipped out and went home. By the time Minnie reached home, the girls were there. She was thankful that all was well, but they each got a good spanking.

Paul was not much of a carpenter, so when he spoke of building his own house across town, Minnie knew that it could be a disaster. As fall arrived, they decided that maybe a real carpenter was needed to begin work on the house. A man named Pat Young was asked to come and look the situation over to see what he thought. He said that he would build the house, but the basement hole was not quite big enough. The dimensions were not really correct, but he said that there was a new way to build a basement, which he called "an Iowa basement." That way, it could work the way it was with a little more work. He staked out a trench 4 feet beyond the existing hole and said that a trench should be dug 3 feet down, and the cement would be poured in the trench.

It wasn't long before Paul had the trench dug. In late September, Pat Young came and built forms that would be filled with cement. By October, when the winter freeze came, the floor was built, and nothing more could be done until spring. It would be another long winter in the shacks for Paul and Minnie and their growing family. Would there be another indoor snowbank again this winter?

During this time of the year, Paul found odd jobs, along with his work at the garage, such as working on frozen pipes, dynamiting rocks and tree stumps, cutting down trees, and preparing logs for the heating stove, as well as any other work he could find. On days when it snowed, he shoveled driveways and walks. He was always busy. He even worked some on the land and basement. However, trying to do much tiling during the bitter cold when the ground was frozen to a depth of 3 feet was virtually impossible to do. The long lengths of tiling would have required using a pickaxe for every foot dug because it was all done by hand with a spade and shovel. There were always many rods—16 1/2 feet—to dig when tiling out a field. It was back breaking work even when the ground wasn't frozen.

Chapter 26

April of 1941 was beautiful, and Pat Young arrived to begin building the walls of the house. He placed the two-by-fours 2 feet apart, and the outside walls were up in almost no time at all. There was no blueprint. His only guide was what Paul and Minnie had described to him, and the size and completion were contingent on how much money he was allotted, which would include his wages. He did have a helper, especially when it came to placing rafters.

Pat began work on the rafters during the time when Minnie was having a difficult time with her pregnancy. He had most of them in place before Minnie got there that weekend. She was shocked. The roof was not anything like she had envisioned. To her chagrin, the roof that should have been facing North and south was actually facing east and west. Pat said that he thought it looked better that way. Minnie was disappointed, but she accepted it, especially since she knew that making him change it would cost time and money, and she wanted to be in the house when winter came.

She would often mention the wrong direction of the roof until the day she died. Paul's biggest priority was to dig a hole and build a better outhouse now that the family would be there more of the time than at the old place. Even his "better" was not at all good, however. Paul certainly proved that he was not a carpenter, but he did possess many other talents. The best was that he was a hard worker. He hardly ever sat down, except to eat, and was always doing something. If he did sit down, he would fall asleep almost instantly. He had a heart of gold that reached to everyone no matter who they were, where they came from, or the color of their skin. And he had musical talent that always made people happy.

Pat Young was a patient man and was confident in his work. With the children around much of the time, he watched his language. He was always laughing, and he sang a tune or two as he worked. He tried to get Pauline and Wilma to sing as he worked. He loved to hear them sing, and he was present when the family performed at the Welcome Inn on the weekends. He would tease the girls to get them to sing and had his pet names for them. Wilma was called "fat cheeks," which she hated. Pauline was called "glasses." Neither girl liked it, but if they responded by singing a song, he stopped his teasing for a while. The two girls sang in harmony, even as young as they were.

By May, Paul and Minnie decided to move the shack that was their kitchen onto the new property to the north of the ongoing building project. It had been a makeshift trailer house before it had been attached to the other shack anyway. With Paul's access to the wrecker from Kyle's Chevy Garage, where he worked, it was a rather easy task. The door that led to the bedroom and living area was made into an outside door. They went back to the old place at night to sleep.

By summertime, Minnie was at the new place more than the old. She wanted her new baby—due sometime in September—to be born in the new house. By August, the two rooms to the north were completed enough so that the family could sleep there. The kitchen and dining rooms were still being worked on. Minnie insisted that the inside walls be plywood throughout the house. She hated the plaster walls that she grew up in. She said that they were too hard and cold. It also was quicker to complete that way. Soon the stove was placed in the new house. Now Minnie could move into her new kitchen.

Florence was right there in the midst of things. She was there with Minnie every step of the way. One day, Florence confided in Minnie that she, too, was pregnant, and she was hoping for a girl this time. Butchie was growing like a weed and was a big helper to his mom. She would come over with Butchie in tow and help as much as she could. She kept having misgivings about her situation. She was reluctant to tell Chuck that she was pregnant because she was afraid of what he might do. She also knew that something was not feeling right about it all.

She was so hoping that this child would be a girl. She always wanted to have a little girl with dark hair like her own. As she was walking home, she began daydreaming about the little girl she wished for so terribly. She yearned for a little girl. She went home thinking of how to create the little dresses she would begin designing as soon as she got home. With Minnie's expert help, she knew she could get it done.

Florence's war was about to become ever more explosive. Chuck was not finished with her yet. This was not going to be the dream of her life. This was not going to be the beautiful little girl she was hoping for. Fortunately, she was oblivious to what lay ahead.

It was the summer of 1941, and the war in Europe was getting worse. Already on June 4, 1940, English soldiers were retreating from the Germans to the area of Dunkirk. There, every English ship, boat, or anything that could float was working to take them back across the English Channel to safety. Miraculously, they were quite successful in doing so. It was a bleak time for the allies. English shipping was taking a beating from the Germans, and nothing was looking positive for the allies at all.

War, of any kind, is a terrible thing. So many innocent people are killed and maimed in addition to the souls that are in the military. This world war was going to be the deadliest war ever. Millions of people were to die, and it would not be the last war. But if America had not entered the war, freedom as we know it would not exist.

Chapter 27

Florence was always a dreamer. After returning home from Minnie's, she fixed a meal for Butchie and herself. He was such a good little guy, and she adored him. As she sat daydreaming in the kitchen after putting him to bed, Chuck came in from a run. He ate some of the meat and potatoes that were leftover from the small evening meal she had put together earlier. She had no idea that he was coming in that night. He complained that there was not enough to fill him up. After yelling to her about it, he left to get "better grub than you will ever be able to fix" and slammed the door as he left. Florence was cramping some, so she was glad to just go to bed.

She fell asleep dreaming of her precious dark-headed little girl. She had left the door unlocked so Chuck could come in when he decided to come home. She was raised to lock her doors in Indiana. However, it was not unusual to leave a door unlocked in this little town of Parkersburg. Very few people ever locked their doors. This was true even when they would be out of town for some time. Cars were always unlocked with the keys in them. There were no break-ins. There was no crime of any kind, except, of course, the times when there was verbal and physical abuse against women in their own homes from their own husbands.

Chuck didn't come home that night or the next day. Florence was not feeling at all well. She stayed in the house, and she had all she could do to take care of Butchie. Minnie came over to see how she was doing, and she noticed that something didn't seem quite right about it all. She took Butchie home with her, and when Paul came home for lunch, she asked him to see if he could find out where Chuck was. Paul knew immediately where to go and ask. The men of a small town always know what is going on. Most people blame women for gossip, but it is usually the men that spread rumors. At least, they always somehow seem to know what's happening.

As Paul came into the restaurant, he asked if anyone had seen Chuck around anywhere that day or the night before. One of the girls on the evening shift said that he was still in the restaurant when she left at 10:30 p.m. She went to ask her boss, Etta.

When Etta came out of the kitchen, she said that Chuck had left on a run to Moline and wouldn't be back until the next night.

Paul stopped at Florence's and saw her in the fetal position on the floor. She looked awful. At first, Paul was afraid that she was dead. When she opened her eyes, he got her up in a chair first. Then he picked her up and laid her on the bed. He noticed a few blood drops on the bed. He went home and told Minnie about the situation. He needed to get back to work, so he brought Minnie over to help Florence.

"I'm afraid that she is going to lose this baby, so she needs to stay in bed as quietly as possible," Minnie said. "On your way to work, would you stop at Doc. Bruechardt's and ask him to come by when he is free?"

"Yeah, I'll do dat. Take care of her and take care of yourself, too," he flung over his shoulder.

As Minnie thought about it, she was really afraid for Florence. She tried to keep all four children as quiet as possible as she went about trying to prepare an evening meal from what little was in Florence's cupboard. She found some flour and enough ingredients to make biscuits. With that, along with some butter and milk, they would have biscuits and gravy. That could fill them up.

It was about four in the afternoon when the doctor came to the door. He examined Florence and then said, "This woman needs to go to the hospital. Where is her husband?"

"God only knows," Minnie replied. "If she needs to go, she needs to go. Which hospital do you think is the best one and the easiest to get to?"

"Allen Memorial Hospital in Waterloo is where I send all my patients. Better yet, I will take her there myself. I'll go to my office and have my wife, who is a great nurse herself, man the office while I'm gone. I'll be back shortly."

Out the door he went. Minnie had never seen him walk that quickly.

It was less than twenty minutes when he was back. Minnie and old Dr. Bruechardt got her into the car, and she was on her way to the hospital. It would take about an hour to get there. The road between Parkersburg and Waterloo was gravel in the Grundy County part, and it was narrow with several curves—one of which was called dead man's curve. It was not much of a curve, but it fools everyone because the road appears to be straight. There was no speed limit at that time except "reasonable and proper," and if one was not careful, that curve could be easily missed, and the ditch was very deep. To this day, the memorials for the dead are still numerous at that spot.

Paul stopped at Florence's house when he finished work. Minnie's baking powder biscuits and white gravy hit the spot. Minnie cleaned everything so that it would be neat as a pin when Florence returned. Then they all went home.

Little Butchie was not a happy little guy without his mommy and in a different bed. Minnie had just gotten him settled with Vern in his bed when suddenly there was a loud banging on the door. Minnie heard, "Where the hell is my family? Where is Florence? I want my supper! What have you done with her, bitch?" This was directed at Minnie.

Paul was out of his chair in a split second and grabbed Chuck by the shirt and held him fast. Through clenched teeth, Paul fairly spat the words, "You don't deserve such a good family. If you vunt to know, Florence may be dead for all vee know. She's in the hospital in Vaterloo, so get your lazy ass movin' and get dere. You might be lucky enough to still see her alive, you son of a bitch."

"Where? What now?" Chuck stammered.

"Get in your damn truck and get da hell to Allen Memorial, you know da place. Take care of your vife!" Paul yelled as Chuck went out the door. Chuck left with wheels spinning.

First, he stopped at his parent's house to tell them what was happening and asked them to call the hospital to tell them he was on his way. They were one of the few families in town that actually had a phone, but it was a party line with several other people in town on the same line. The Millers were quite a bit better off than many of the people in Parkersburg. They happened to own about 40 acres, along with the house and barn by the Catholic cemetery. His mom balked a little because it was long distance and would be expensive to call. Chuck insisted that his mom call the hospital to tell them that he was on his way and that he would not give permission to do surgery or anything else until he got there and signed for it. His first thought was "Now I wonder how much this is going to cost me."

As he drove, he wondered what he would find when he got to the hospital. He secretly hoped that Florence was dead. If she was, then he could have his life back just like he always had before all this stuff with Florence happened. He said to himself, "My parents can take care of the brat. They always wanted grandchildren anyway, and I can live like I want to. Nobody can stop me. Yeah." He smiled smugly to himself.

Chapter 28

Chuck slammed the door of the truck and ran to the door of the hospital. He was stopped at the front desk and sent to the second floor, where Florence had been prepped for surgery. She was already under the anesthetic when Chuck got there.

The doctor spoke to him briefly and explained to him that Florence was pregnant and that the baby was developing in the fallopian tube, which had burst. He must remove the tube as quickly as possible. Of course, the baby would not survive, but it would save Florence.

After the shock of learning of Florence's pregnancy and this turn of events, he listened carefully. As the doctor explained the procedure, Chuck became aware for the first time of the workings of a woman's body. He had no idea how everything came about to bring a child into the world. He just didn't care and really didn't even want to know. He never really understood how a child was conceived, how it all progressed, and how things can easily go awry. His mind was working quickly now. Even in the 1940s, many women died in the process of childbirth, and a situation like this was especially dangerous. It was said that every time a woman went through childbirth that she was "walking through the valley of the shadow of death." That was always in their minds as women brought life into the world in those days. Yet it still happens even in the twenty-first century. There are no certainties in any of it.

Chuck's first question to the doctor was "Will she still be able to have kids after this?"

The surgeon answered quickly because he was needed in surgery, "Yes, it is possible, because a woman has two fallopian tubes."

"Two?" Chuck fairly shouted. Chuck was now ready to blow and out came "So then take the other tube out too. I don't want to take care of any more squallin' brats. We already have one, and I didn't want him. I still don't, but now I'm stuck."

The doctor was shocked at that, but he also knew that he had no choice but to do what the husband wanted, or he could possibly be sued or even lose his license to practice medicine. He also had no time to argue. In order to get Chuck to sign the admission papers and agree to pay the bill, he had little choice. It might already be too late. At that time in history, a married woman had no say over her own body. The man owned her just like he did a house or car or a dog. Women had no say about anything. It was perfectly legal for Chuck to insist and demand his rights as the husband.

The surgery went quite well, and Florence came through in fairly good shape. With the tube having burst, it took some time to get it all cleaned out. Chuck did stay until she woke up. Florence was happy that he was there, so she didn't feel so alone in a strange place. Florence asked if he would just go home and take care of things there. Maybe in the morning, he could take Butchie to stay with his parents for the time being. He smiled and agreed, satisfied that he was now totally in control and would be from now on.

Florence saw Chuck grin, and she thought it a little strange. *What is with him? Somehow, he seems pleased about something. I hope it is because he actually does care about our son and me. Maybe things will be different. I sure hope so*, she thought as she drifted off into a well-deserved, restful sleep. She smiled as she faded off into oblivion.

Before Chuck left the hospital, he had a private conversation with the doctor to be sure that his plan was carried out. The staff was also alerted that this was to be kept totally quiet. One particular nurse was horrified that the procedure had been done without Florence's knowledge or consent. She was forced to keep it quiet even though she knew it wasn't morally right. This was the first time in all her years of nursing that she actually realized that women didn't have the right to have control over what happened to their own bodies. This was especially true of married women. As Nurse Newgard thought about all the times women were brought in beaten, strangled, vaginally and rectally bleeding, and now this horrible situation where Florence had been stripped of her right to bear children, she didn't know if she could continue in her chosen profession—a profession where now she was warned to never tell a patient what happened to her in surgery. She was devastated. She went home to her apartment, thankful that she was not married, especially to such a beast. She thought, *Here he has such a beautiful and good wife, and he does this to her*. Nurse Newgard was crying at the total injustice of it all. Men controlled everything. Women were under the control of the husbands, financially and in every other way. They had no idea that they could make it on their own because, in those days, women stayed home and kept everything going, even when the husbands, who were supposed to be making a living for the family, really didn't always do so. Because of that unwritten law, many women endured horrible living conditions because they were "supposed" to be married and have children.

About a year later, Nurse Newgard quit nursing and was found dead shortly afterward, having killed herself because of the "futility of it all," as her note stated. She knew how to mix the drugs to make herself sleep away to nothingness. This was another case of men's dominance over women. Even in a profession where women could help other women, they were stifled. They couldn't do their jobs properly nor, as in this case, honestly. She had tried to escape from Florence's room every time Florence wanted to talk to her, especially about having more children and how happy she was that she could have children even after this. All this was a lie, and nurse Newgard could not tell her otherwise.

No one told Florence what had transpired, other than that she had what they called an ectopic pregnancy, and because the fallopian tube in which the baby was developing had to be removed, she was no longer pregnant; however, she would be fine. She cried for her lost baby, not realizing that she would never have another. She would never have the large family that she had always dreamed of. This would be the beginning of the avalanche that would bury her. This was a battle that she would never win. Her thought at this time was "I'll never have a loving husband, but if I have a little girl who loves me, I can be happy. Right now, I'm too tired to care."

After two weeks in the hospital, Florence went home.

It was the usual tension-filled house each time Chuck was home. Florence was lucky that her husband was gone on the road most of the time. It was so obvious that he despised her and blamed her for every little thing that happened that he didn't particularly like. She tried her best to appease him and pamper him when he was home in hopes that he would treat her with a little kindness.

One evening, she was writing a letter to her parents when Chuck came home. She did not expect him home that evening. Chuck was furious with her for "wasting" the paper, so he grabbed it from her, slapped her across the face with it, and tore it to shreds. "Now you have nothing to write on. How does that feel, bitch? Now you can't write home to Mama. Ha, Ha! I'll bet you were complaining to them about me. Well, complain all you want, so there. It won't do you any good. Just remember you wouldn't be in this marriage if it weren't for them."

He always would bring that up. She didn't say anything, but she was thinking, *It's not their fault that you raped me.*

At least this time, there was no black eye or cut lip. He then grabbed her, dragged her in the bedroom, and used her to his satisfaction. Afterward, he rolled over and slept.

Florence was thankful that he left early the next morning, and she assumed he was going on a run. She was just happy that he was gone for a while again. She hated being in the same house with him. She was always a nervous wreck when he was home.

Florence went to Minnie's and had coffee. Minnie made the best coffee. Minnie noticed the mark on her cheek but said nothing.

Chapter 29

On September 19, 1941, Minnie had another little girl. They named her Judy Kay. Minnie had a really rough labor giving birth this time. It was five days after her twenty-sixth birthday. Verbena Brown, Abbo's oldest daughter, came and helped the doctor. Since she only lived a short distance away, it was a good choice. Of course, the brothers came and congratulated Paul and Minnie with a schnapps. Although it was not a boy, it was another healthy baby girl. As was the custom, the mother spent ten days in bed. It was difficult for families to manage without the mother for that length of time, especially when there were several small children to take care of in addition to the usual chores. Verbena went every morning to help. Florence was kind to let the children stay at her house for some of that time and to be there when Verbena couldn't be. At the old place, Becky Allison was always there, but now things were different.

Olive Williams also helped out. Minnie was not as strong this time as she had been before and was grateful for the help. When she finally recovered enough to take care of things, she was her old self again except for the terrible pain she had for several days each month. The doctor gave her such strong red pills that her fingernails turned blue/black, especially at the base of the nail. As long as she had the pills, she could take the pain.

Florence was a godsend on those days. She was always close at hand when Minnie needed her. The winter of 1941 was very cold in Iowa. The family was in the new house, so they didn't need to worry about indoor snowbanks accumulating any more. The heater in the living room was the same one taken along from the shacks. It heated the house well. The tar paper under the siding helped to keep out the cold. Siding that was chosen looked like real bricks, and it kept the wind out better than that which the old place had. Everyone appreciated the warm home. Minnie was always making quilts out of small scraps of leftover material that had been used for other projects. These also helped the family stay warm. They were filled with cotton batting—if there was money to purchase some. Otherwise, old blankets that were too worn out to use as blankets were repurposed as filler in the quilts. When a quilt was sewn together on the edges, Minnie took a large needle and tied yarn at various places to keep the makeshift batting from shifting around.

Each time a new baby was born, Minnie made new baby clothes and flannel diapers. Twelve yards of fabric resulted in thirteen diapers—all, of course, sewn and hemmed by hand. She had no sewing machine in those days. Short dresses were made for the baby because if the new baby was a boy, it could be a shirt. If it was a girl, it would work as a dress. Many times, embroidery was also added that could work for either a boy or a girl. There was no way of telling for sure by anyone in those days, even if you had millions of dollars, what the baby's gender would be until it was born. Although they had been hoping for another little boy this time, Minnie's little Judy was nice and cozy in their new home. This was a much better house in which to raise children.

Naturally, there was no bathroom and no water in the house. That fall, Paul had tried his best to dig a well, all to no avail. His attempts were always a failure. This meant that they had to ask their next-door neighbors if they could draw water from their well. This worked out well for the first couple of years.

Of course, Paul continued to try to find water on the property. Here the land had been a water hole and was now mostly fill dirt. It just didn't seem possible that there was not water somewhere on the property. Across the road to the south, there was a spring, but that land was not owned by Paul and Minnie and was not accessible to them. It was fenced in, and it would be impossible to climb the fence with a bucket of water. There was also no faucet. It was simply flowing out of the ground. *Vell, soon comes da vinter again. Maybe I try again next spring,* Paul thought.

Then December 7, 1941, came, and the world came crashing down for everyone.

To Minnie, this seemed appropriately symbolic as she thought about what may lie ahead for her best friend. Florence was married to a man as devious and evil as those who dropped bombs on people who were totally unaware there was even a threat. But Minnie and Florence were both completely unaware of just exactly how devious Chuck really was. Florence had many hard-fought battles, and each one seemed worse than the last one. News of the war only made her think of her own battle-filled life. Her only real joy in life was to be with Minnie and the children. She loved the attention that Minnie's girls gave her. However, when she was home alone, it made her long to have a little girl of her own even more.

Florence had to tread very carefully around Chuck because she never knew when he would strike out because of some imagined infraction. She fought hard to keep the home as safe as possible for her son. She had to keep a close eye on Chuck so that he didn't hurt Butchie. She was always wary and watchful. When someone—or some nation—is untrustworthy, you always need to be on guard. It is even worse when what is happening is evil and is presented as good or Christian or as if "it's their own fault, and they deserve it." Even Hitler was convinced that he was doing the right thing for his country to "get rid of all the undesirables." There is no hope when that attitude becomes the norm.

Chapter 30

When Florence had first come home from the hospital, Minnie went every day to help with everything that needed doing. Sometimes, Minnie took washing home with her and did it in her new basement. Most of the basement was used for storing the potatoes and other vegetables and canned goods that had been made from the vegetables harvested that fall. There was, however, room by the stairs to put a washtub and stand to do the laundry—all by hand, of course. However, since there was electricity in this house, she was just thrilled when, a couple of years later, she got an actual washing machine! The washer had a tub with a dolly that sloshed the clothes back and forth. When the load seemed clean enough, she would take the clothes one by one and put them through the wringer that was mounted on the washer and let them drop into her tub full of cold, clear water. There she pushed them further into the water and moved them up and down to rinse. Then she turned the wringer over the rinse tub so that she could wring the clothes which then would drop in the clothes basket. After that, she would take them out to the line and pin them with clothespins to dry. With electricity, all that was now possible. She also no longer had to use oil lamps here, unless, of course, there were power outages. Each room had a bare bulb in the ceiling for light. The basement did too.

As Florence began to get stronger, she was able to do her own work. Taking care of a small boy was always a challenge. Little Butchie was growing up and talking up a storm by now. He was an active boy. Minnie always brought her children along during the couple of weeks Florence had been in the hospital and then while taking care of her at home afterward. Butchie and Vern were inseparable. Sometimes, Florence would ask if Vern could stay a little longer so that the two boys could play together. That was okay with Minnie, especially if she was sure that Chuck wouldn't show up.

One day, when Florence walked over to Minnie's to have afternoon tea and bring Vern back home, the conversation turned to her losing her baby, and Florence was overcome with grief. Minnie's company always seemed to cheer her. Minnie was sympathetic but always came back with "You are still young, and you can try again."

Florence replied with "That's not what Chuck says. He says that I will never get pregnant again."

Minnie assured her, "Oh yes, you can. A woman has two fallopian tubes. Doc Bruechardt told me so. You normally have two ovaries and two tubes, and only one of your tubes is missing, so if I'm not mistaken, that should mean that you should be able to have another child. Every other month, the ovary on one side produces an egg. The next month, the one on the other side produces one. It goes down to the uterus—that's the womb—where it can be fertilized to produce a child. To get there, it goes through the fallopian tube. You no longer have one of them, so your chances are cut in half. But it should not be impossible."

After Florence left, she felt much better. She was confident that she could have more children. She went home happy.

Minnie had her hands full with getting supper ready, so she wasn't paying much attention to Vern. When she picked him up, she noticed that he had a nice fragrance on him and asked, "Did you have fun at Florence's? Why do you smell so good?"

Vern answered, "Yeah, we had fun. We puayed dress up. Do you have any yiptick?"

Minnie asked, "You mean lipstick?"

Vern nodded.

Minnie responded, "No, I can't afford lipstick."

Vern answered, "Well, Foince have some. I yike yiptick. It feels good. It is purty too."

Minnie replied, "So that is why you smell so good. She must have put some perfume on you too. I think that we should wash you up a little before your dad gets home. Boys don't usually wear lipstick, but if it feels good, that's fine. I see that you must have had candy, too, because you are a little sticky."

Minnie thought about Florence and how she longed for a little girl which was probably the reason she played dress up with the two boys. It would soon be getting cold, and the boys would not have many chances to be together. It was a good three-block walk between houses, but this was better than walking across town like they used to do before the new house went up. Minnie was expecting another child that September. She and Paul hoped for another boy so that Vern would have a playmate.

Minnie and Paul were saving money to buy a radio. They felt that with the war already raging in Europe, it would be good to keep up on the world news. Paul rigged a wire up along the side of the house for an aerial. He did not like to be on a ladder, so Minnie climbed up and ran the wire along the eaves. She was never afraid of heights. She had helped shingle the roof a couple of months before and never gave it a thought. On the other hand, Paul could dig into the ground to almost any depth and not have any qualms about it. He did experience a few cave-ins during his work on tiling, water-lines, and sewer projects, but he could always get out before he was totally covered. However, up on a ladder was not his thing at all. He hated heights.

Minnie could do just about anything. She could do electrical work and most anything else that needed doing. Paul was not really adept at those kinds of things. Paul was a musician, expert at tiling, and was able to see "fall" on a tiling project without any kind of surveyor's tools.

He was an expert driver, too, never having had an accident during his entire life. He could fix any automobile and created his own machines to do outdoor work. He used an old car, cut the back off behind the driver's seat, kept the chassis, and made a box, so he had a pickup. He made his own "saw outfit," he called it, again made from a car chassis with the whole body cut off. Keeping the drive train intact, he attached a huge round saw blade, which he used to cut tree trunks into pieces for firewood to heat the house in winter. The old cars around the house were left there by Paul's boss, Vern Kyle, to be junked out. Paul utilized them to create his new machines.

Their new toy, the radio, was a godsend for getting the world news. Being able to actually hear the voice of the president of the United States was a totally new experience. With the radio installed properly, the sound was heavenly. They listened to President Roosevelt as he gave his fireside speeches. It was like he was right there with them talking to them personally. He had first served as president in 1933—the same year that Adolph Hitler was voted in as chancellor of Germany. The entire world had experienced the Great Depression, which began when the stock market crashed in 1929, during the time when a Republican from Iowa, Herbert Hoover, was president. Apparently, he had no idea as to how to bring it to a halt.

As soon as Roosevelt was elected, he started changing things for the better. People were put back to work through the New Deal's public works program building roads, bridges, dams, park facilities, and more. FDR also gave us Social Security, which has saved many people from becoming destitute in their older age. His wife Eleanor even went into the shantytowns, tent cities, and Hoovervilles herself to find out how things could be improved. And things did begin to turn around. Factories sprang up. Lives were changed. Many of the people who were living during this time will attest to Mrs. Roosevelt's influence, and everyone loved the president for what he did for the country.

Interestingly, the first time Roosevelt ran, Paul was not yet a naturalized citizen and, therefore, could not vote. But Minnie could since women had finally won that right in August of 1920. The day she went to cast her first vote for Roosevelt, however, the workers at the polling station would not allow her to vote, even though she was born in America. She had even brought her birth certificate to prove it. They told her that since she was married to an "alien," they couldn't let her vote. Outraged, the ever spunky and feisty Minnie decided to write a letter directly to President Roosevelt, and to her great delight, he answered her with a personal letter in return! After that, she always took that letter with her every time she voted, even after Paul became eligible. After Paul became a naturalized citizen, he always voted, and he always brought his citizenship papers along with him. He and Minnie both voted for President Roosevelt every time he ran.

In November of 1941, Roosevelt ran for an unprecedented third term as president. This had never happened before. An unspoken tradition had been set by George Washington that a president might choose to run for a second term after winning a first, and subsequent presidents had generally followed that example. Though they didn't always win a second time, most Americans felt that one or two terms served was the norm. This time, however, with war looming on the horizon, the American people actually drafted Roosevelt to run because they felt that war was almost a certainty, and Franklin Roosevelt was the person with the most experience in leadership at the time. He chose Henry Wallace to be his running mate. Of course, Roosevelt won by a landslide.

Having elected Roosevelt to a third term was a very good choice, as it turned out, after Japan, with no provocation or warning, destroyed our naval base and airfield at Pearl Harbor, where most of the US Navy ships were tied up. That surprise attack changed the entire nature and scope of the war, and President Roosevelt was just the man to lead America through the devastation of another World War.

Paul and Minnie sat in shock on that horrific Sunday when Pearl Harbor was bombed. This would be a day no one would ever forget. Minnie's first concern was her brother Ray, who had enlisted in 1939 and was serving at Pearl Harbor. Paul and Minnie decided that the next Sunday, they would go to Waterloo to see her mom and stepdad. Hopefully, they would have some word of Ray's plight. In this instance, it might be weeks before they would hear anything, but at least they would try.

When they arrived in Waterloo the following week, Lena was consumed with worry and fear. She hadn't heard anything, and even though she lived in the city, she still had no telephone. Paul and Minnie had no phone either. That is how it was in 1941. Telephones were for the rich.

When they left Lena's house on that December 14, 1941, to travel back home, everyone seemed worn out. The winter storms raged, and it was not until the end of January 1942 that Lena received a telegram informing her that Ray was in the hospital in Honolulu, receiving medical aid for his burns and a broken leg. When his ship was hit, the deck gave way, and he fell below, breaking his leg. When he escaped the ship he was on, he was burned in the water, where the leaking fuel from the ships had been ignited in the attack.

It wasn't until several months later that Lena and Minnie each received letters from Ray telling them that he would be laid up for quite some time, but that he would recover and "not to worry!" Minnie was happy to hear from her brother, and she seemed to be a bit more at ease after reading the letter. Ray stayed in the Navy throughout the war and later on became a chief petty officer.

Now the war effort began in full force. Everything stopped to build war-making matériel, this time for our own military. Detroit stopped making automobiles and changed instead to building tanks, jeeps, bombs—anything and everything that was needed for all-out war. The country was entirely focused on winning the war, and everyone contributed in some way to help reach that goal. It didn't matter whether it was building ships, submarines, airplanes, ammunition, guns, or whether it was planting crops to feed the soldiers, sailors, marines, coast guardsmen, Seabees, nurses, WACS, WAVES, WASPS. Parachutes and uniforms needed to be sewn, packages needed to be shipped, and everyone was helping to provide all the things necessary to keep the fighting men supplied with the things they needed in order to carry on their responsibilities of winning the war. The people at home sacrificed like they never had before. Some things simply were not available until the war was over. It was virtually impossible to get a new car until after the war. Farmers were given some leeway, however, and they were able to get most of the gas they needed to plant and harvest crops. Of course, some farmers were still using horses, but it was slowly changing.

Women were hired in the factories to build planes, ships, tanks, and other equipment. They went gladly to help build the essential equipment needed to carry on the war and to bring it to a close. To some women, it was a rude awakening when the war was over and the factories didn't need them anymore because when the men came home from the war, they needed those jobs. But most of the women liked what they were doing, and they liked receiving a paycheck that they could use as they saw fit. The term "Rosie the Riveter" came about as a symbol of the women who created many of the weapons of war. Rivets were used on much of the equipment, especially airplanes.

Men were drafted into military service, so women offered their services not only here at home but also in the Army, Navy, Air Force, and anywhere else they could help. Nurses volunteered, and virtually, everyone, even the children, contributed what they could. Every child in school was taught to save string, peel the aluminum foil off the gum wrappers, sort scrap, and save anything that could be used in any way for the war effort. Nothing was wasted, and children were involved nearly as much as the adults were.

In school, every morning, after singing the "Star-Spangled Banner" and saying the Pledge of Allegiance to the flag, a prayer was led by the teacher for war's end and victory over evil.

Rationing stamp books were a must. You could not buy sugar, coffee, shoes, tires, or any other such luxuries without them. The stamps were given out according to how many people were in the family, and everyone needed stamps in addition to money to buy most of the necessities. People would trade rationing stamps among themselves to get more of what they needed and less of what they didn't. When there were not enough stamps for the family to get what they needed the most, they simply traded with other people for the stamps those people wanted in return. Since Minnie and Paul didn't need the liquor stamps, for example, they traded those to Paul's brothers in exchange for coffee, sugar and other canning supplies for Minnie, and necessities such as gasoline that Paul needed for his work. The items that were rationed with stamps were the very things that were sent to those who were actually fighting the war.

Many things were changed by the war. Everyone was told to have dark shades on their windows for blackouts. These blackouts were common during WWII. Every town, no matter how small, had to do frequent blackout drills. When the siren blared any night of the week, all the lights in town had to be turned off. This served as practice so that if a bombing or invasion from the enemy were to take place, everyone would be prepared to darken the city. From the air, you would not be able to see that there was a town at that location at night. Sometimes, you could hear the airplanes overhead, checking to make sure that everything was dark. If you needed a light to see so that you would be safe to move about your house, you had to pull the blackout shades down over the windows to make sure no light escaped. No peeking was permitted.

Even the little town of Parkersburg observed these blackouts. The patrol cars that were put in charge of the success of this practice would drive around town, moving slowly past each house, checking to make certain that everyone was following the blackout rules. If you did not follow them properly, you were given a tag to remedy whatever was not up to par so that the offender would come into compliance with the rules. At Paul and Minnie's house, it was usually that the shade was not all the way down because of the curiosity of the little ones.

There were official vehicles around town with listening devices that checked to see if there were any spies. This was especially true in Parkersburg because there were so many German immigrants there. One family was especially plagued by the car on the street in front of their house. Many people in America today are unaware that a great many German immigrants and people of German descent were held in holding camps until the war was over, as were many Japanese. This is a natural outcome of war and of being suspicious of everyone. Those of German descent accepted this but were very apprehensive when the war was won, and the concentration camps in Germany were discovered. The fear of retaliation was very real, even though the Germans in America had nothing to do with that horrific situation. Of course, they were all welcome to return home after the war; however, it was not always a pleasant experience and even less so at war's end. Many times, their homes had been sold, and they had to start over. Yet most were still happy to be in America where it was easier to start over.

It was very difficult to be alive during the war, even though there were few actual attacks on home soil. However, there are many things that came to light after the war ended that had taken place here in America. In Hawaii, for example, some Japanese sympathizers had actually cut arrows in their fields to show where Pearl Harbor and the airfield were located. There were many spies in Hawaii that were discovered during the war, later in the war, and after the war.

The Japanese also used balloons to send toward our Western shores. There were a number of fires in the Western Mountains caused by balloons with explosive devices, and one balloon even went as far as Colorado and left a huge crater there after its explosive device detonated. Of course, all this was explained away by Washington to keep the populace from becoming too alarmed. Nothing of this was in the news at the time but was declassified years later after the war was long over.

On the home front, America was very aware of the possibility that there could be attacks on our home soil. At that time, Hawaii was not yet a state nor was Alaska—Alaska didn't become a state until 1949 and Hawaii not until 1950. There were Japanese encampments on the Aleutian Islands, and there was a campaign by Americans to bring those islands back under American control starting in June 1942 through August of 1943. The American continent was not safe from attack by the Japanese with their submarines and balloons or the Germans with their Unterseeboots—undersea boats commonly known as U-boats. It was a very apprehensive and dangerous time in history. Nothing or no one was really safe. The least safe of all was Florence.

Chapter 31

By April of 1942, Americans were morally discouraged. There were no victories as yet because America had not been prepared for war. Prior to December of 1941, America had been assisting England and her allies by producing war matériel. Some American men went to Canada to enlist so they could help the situation in England, but the US was not officially involved until after Pearl Harbor. By 1942, soldiers and sailors began being dispersed to European and Pacific theaters of war. Although American soldiers and sailors were in both theaters of war, there were no significant victories.

By April 10, 1942, America learned that some Americans and Filipinos had been captured by the Japanese and that the Bataan Death March took place. They had made the mistake of surrendering to the Japanese. In short, one thousand Americans and nine thousand Filipinos died. It was a sixty-six-mile trek. They were made to march with no water or food in intense heat while being tortured along the way. When the injured could go no further, they were either killed or left to die where they fell, unless their fellow prisoners tried to help them, placing their own lives in danger. It was totally inhumane and certainly against the Geneva Convention, which had been drafted to prevent just such horror against mankind.

Americans needed something big to happen to bring some sort of hope to the situation. The Axis powers—Germany, Japan, and Italy—were claiming more and more of the world, and as they conquered more and more territory, the people of the invaded country were expected to become part of the mind and strength of those in power. If there was resistance, those resisting would simply be killed or placed in concentration camps. The tyrants—Hitler, Mussolini, Hirohito, Tojo, Yamamoto, and others—would use their power any way they chose in order to make sure that there was no resistance.

America needed a morale booster, and a pilot named Jimmy Doolittle was just the man to do it. As one of the greatest pilots of this time, Jimmy came up with a brainstorm to bomb the homeland of the Japanese. Of course, the war department had much difficulty asking anyone to risk their lives on such a scheme. Therefore, he asked for volunteers to help bomb Japan. Every airman knew that there were no airplanes at that time that could make that distance and get anywhere to safety before the fuel ran out. Jimmy had no problem getting volunteers, however, even though no bomber had ever taken off from an aircraft carrier prior to that time. As most bombers were too heavy and cumbersome to take off from a carrier, he chose B25s to do the job. His idea worked, and by April, his plan was in force.

On April 18, 1942, bombs rained down on the Japanese homeland. However, there had been a hitch that had not been expected—the aircraft carriers were spotted by some Japanese fishing boats. Doolittle knew they would warn Japan that bombers were on their way. He knew he had to get the planes off the decks and in the air before the warlords in Japan could be warned. Because they were farther away than planned, this meant that they would certainly run out of fuel, but hopefully, after the bombing, they would utilize some other options that had been discussed at the briefings. Their bombers had to be either ditched in the ocean or landed in China with the help of Chinese friends, some of whom even made makeshift landing strips for them. These friends also helped shelter the airmen. Unfortunately, some of their villages were burned to the ground, and many people were killed and tortured by the Japanese in an effort to capture the airmen. Even Chinese women and children were tortured and killed by the Japanese in their determination to find the Americans.

All this was top secret. Only those directly involved knew what was going on. Some of the volunteers lost their lives on this raid, but this daring deed was successful, at least as far as demoralizing Japan. The Japanese now knew that they could be attacked by American bombers. But most of all, this mission gave Americans the hope that was so badly needed—that this dreaded war might be able to be won after all. Now they felt that Pearl Harbor was at least somewhat vindicated.

The next victory came on June 4, 1942, when the battle of Midway took place. It was a miraculous victory for the allies that was unexpected by those who were involved because this small task force knew that they had a much smaller group of ships compared to the superior feet of Japanese. This unexpected victory gave Americans more hope for total victory and the war's end.

Every evening at the supper table, the Waterloo Courier was read to the children at Paul and Minnie's house concerning the war, as well as other news of local interest. Especially important to them was news of local soldiers and sailors. Those who were lost or wounded in the war were named and listed in the paper, along with their rank, and if it was known and not classified, the theater of war, and the general area where they lost their lives or were wounded.

Abbo's two sons, Jake and Bert, joined the Navy and went to training at the Great Lakes Training Station. Another local young man, Bill Card, went into the Marines. It seemed like every family was affected somehow. Paul's brother, John's son, John Jr., went into the Army and, ironically, served in Germany as well as other parts of Europe. Many men went voluntarily to get the war over sooner, and some were drafted. At the same time war was raging in Europe, Minnie's cousin was drafted and went into the Army Air Force. He became a tail gunner in a B17 over Europe.

It was during this time that Paul's mother Alice received a letter informing her that her daughter Angel's house in Northern Germany was accidently bombed by a crippled B17, which had been dropping bombs to lighten the load in an effort to get back across the English Channel to land in England. Although Angel's home had not been a target, she was killed. No one found out whether or not the plane made it back to a landing field in England. Of course, the letter had been opened before it ever was delivered to Parkersburg. It appeared that it had come by an English ship to New York. How it actually made it to America during wartime no one could answer because security was so tight.

Of course, all Paul could do was rant and rave about Hitler and how he wished "dat SOB would be killed soon." "Da sooner, da better," he said. He was good at swearing in three languages. This was the perfect opportunity to do so. Angel had always been his favorite sibling because she tried to take care of him when his folks left him in Germany at age nine. Now she was dead because of that bastard Hitler. Paul always went to her as a young man, but it was a long walk. He was an indentured servant—in other words, a slave to the farmer he worked for. He received no pay except for being given a straw bed in the barn and very little food. Naturally, there was never any hope of going to Germany for a funeral, even if there had been no war. It was simply a matter of money. There was never enough of it.

With all these things on his mind after learning of Angel's death, Paul had difficulty sleeping. His thoughts went back to the misery he had in Germany. He was always cold there. He said many times that the only brightness he had being of the lower class in Germany was his joy with his sister Angel. He never blamed his parents for leaving him there at such a young age. He was genuinely a happy person. He never held a grudge, and he never considered himself poor. Though he had very few material things, even in America, he was a grateful person. He owned a piece of ground—about an acre—where he had a bountiful garden, a cow for milk and butter, a few chickens, and usually a hog for meat. He built a home, had a family, and in his own words, he always had "plenty." He had enough to eat and a bed to sleep in, and he was a thankful and happy man.

Paul and all his brothers got together to mourn Angel's passing. It was a good thing because they could express their mutual grief, which made things a little easier. Paul, especially, was having a tough time accepting Angel's death, but when he began singing and playing the accordion, he perked up a bit. The very act of playing music and singing some of the old German songs, along with a few country songs from the radio, made all of them realize that life would go on. As his brother Joe would say, "That's life."

On November 13, 1942, the USS *Juneau CL52* was hit by a Japanese torpedo and sank, killing 687 US sailors. Among them were the five Sullivan brothers—the very Sullivan brothers that were Minnie's childhood friends. Their parents, Tom and Aleta Sullivan, received the news when three Naval officers came to their home. It was the hardest thing these officers ever had to do. When Tom was about to open the door to go to work on the Illinois Central Railroad, he saw a naval officer coming up to the house and knew it was going to be bad by the officer's sad look. Tom asked, "Which one?"

The naval officer replied, "All five." George age twenty-seven, Francis age twenty-five, Joseph age twenty-three, Madison age twenty-two, and Albert age nineteen. Had there been more US ships in the area at the time, some of the crew might have been saved. In retrospect, it was amazing that there were as many ships as there were, with the fleet having been almost decimated at Pearl Harbor. The ships that were brought back to the surface took many months of intensive repair before they could become usable again.

No one could understand how those unfortunate parents were able to withstand such a monumental loss. The tragedy of losing all five sons at once was unimaginable to all those who heard the horrible news. Yet only a few months later, Tom and Aleta agreed to go on tour to promote the cause of building more ships by asking people to buy war bonds so that more ships could be built and possibly avoid another such catastrophe. It was a testament to their strength and resolve and seemed to be their way of honoring their sons.

When Minnie heard the news, she was absolutely devastated. She kept saying, "How can this be? They were together to keep each other safe. My god, I can't believe it!" She could not be consoled. It was weeks before she could stop crying. This was a terrible blow to her. For the rest of her life, she would occasionally talk about it with her three older children, who were there when she got the news. The tears would always flow again. It never seemed to leave her.

One day, while reflecting on the loss and grief she was feeling because of the war, it suddenly occurred to Minnie that every battle that was fought in World War II seemed to parallel Florence's life of personal battles in some way. Minnie likened those battles that took place before the United States became involved in the war to a foreshadowing of the turmoil that was brewing before Florence ever even realized that her marriage would ultimately become a warzone. Florence's innocence was destroyed by Chuck, just like the United States' innocence was lost by the utter destruction of Pearl Harbor, when the devastation of war became real. When Minnie's friends— the five Sullivan brothers—perished at sea, it was as if Florence's hopes for another child perished along with them. "The *Juneau* going down was just like Florence's spirit being sunk to the bottom of the sea," she mused. During the Battle of Leyte Gulf in which the Americans first witnessed a kamikaze pilot sacrifice himself, Minnie thought of how Florence's life was purposely shattered by her husband with no regard for her at all, causing Florence to feel she had nothing left to live for. And finally, with the battle of Iwo Jima, Minnie felt a foreboding that haunted her for the rest of her life. "I fear this is not going to end well," she said to herself.

Chapter 32

The war continued to rage on, and the American people continued to pray for the war to be over, but the Germans were advancing steadily, and it seemed that they were not being stopped. Even though they had signed the nonaggression pact with the Soviet Union on August 23, 1939, Germany invaded that country in June of 1941.

The German war machine had invaded Poland in 1939 and conquered everything in its path. Numerous major battles and events took place before the US declared war in December 1941 and throughout the remainder of the war. At least twenty of those were given special names.[3] A battle has to be significant to earn a name. These battles caused the people of the United States to realize that the war would certainly be lost without our active participation. Of course, as a war goes on, there is a constant battle until the war is declared over.

There were still Japanese in the tunnels and caves long after the major battle was over. They continued to be sought after because they caused trouble for the Americans stationed there throughout the length of the war. Iwo Jima, an island of approximately 8 square miles, became an air base close enough to Japan to use the B29s. The island was ultimately taken from the Japanese, but it took over a month of intense fighting. Six thousand eight hundred Americans were killed there. That amounts to 850 deaths per square mile. It had been shelled by the US Navy prior to the landing, though the

---

[3] See Appendix for a list of the major named battles.

shelling didn't do much good, it seems, because the landing that first day took the lives of two thousand marines.

On July 30, 1945, the USS *Indianapolis* was on its way back from the airfield on the island of Tinian, where the ship had delivered parts of what would become the first atomic bomb. The ship was torpedoed by a Japanese submarine, and with the bow completely torn off, it sank in twelve minutes. There were three hundred men who went down with the ship. The remaining nine hundred found themselves struggling to survive in shark-infested waters, where six hundred more died trying to stay alive. Finally, on August 2, 1945, the remaining sailors were rescued by Lieutenant Wilber "Chuck" Gwinn and copilot Lieutenant Warren Colwell in a PVI Ventura aircraft. They had been in the Philippine Sea on their way to the Philippines. This was the largest loss of life at sea in the history of the US Navy.

Americans had lived through an intense, costly, devastatingly long war, and the people just wanted it over with. American people gave their all during this war. It was the worst war ever fought because the entire world was at war. It touched everyone.

It is amazing that America was involved by a declaration only from December 7, 1941, to May 8, 1945, in Europe and August 14 or 15, 1945, when Japan finally signed the peace treaty. That amounts to three years and four months to conquer Europe and three years and seven months to conquer Japan. In comparison to some later wars, it was not terribly long, especially for a world war raging in so many places. It was truly amazing. For a people who did not want war, when the stakes were high, Americans did everything possible to get it over with as quickly as possible.

The one ultimate blow that finally brought the war to a close over Japan was the fact that America was working on a bomb that was so powerful that it could disintegrate most of a city in a single strike. The only way that the Japanese would capitulate would be to drop one of these. It was called an atomic bomb. America also developed a heavy bomber aircraft to carry this bomb to its destination. It was called a B-29, and it was the most technically advanced of any bomber ever made at the time—the newest generation long-range heavy bomber of its day. However, it had not had years of testing like the B17s had, so during the plane's operational testing in 1942, several engine design flaws made the B-29 prone to engine fires while performing power checks on the runway and sometimes shortly after takeoff. Unfortunately, those problems were never adequately resolved until after the war. Because of this flaw, the pilots refused to fly them—especially after Edmund T. Allen "Eddie," a renowned test pilot for Boeing, perished when one of the engines on the B29 he was testing caught fire. Allen, eight crew members, and nineteen civilians on the ground were killed when the plane crashed into a meat-packing plant. The plane had four Wright engines, and the men joked, "No, they are wrong engines."

In the meantime, in November of 1944, President Roosevelt ran for a fourth term and won again. He chose Harry Truman from Independence, Missouri, as his running mate. Harry had very little time as vice president because Roosevelt died in April of 1945.

The war department kept pressing to get the pilot program going in earnest, but without pilots to fly the B29, the atomic bomb project would not happen. Finally, Lt. Col. Paul Tibbets was given the task. One of the true stories connected with this new state-of-the-art bomber is that the pilots who were to fly these monsters were supposed to be men. To show these men that the B29 was both safe and reliable, he decided to get women to fly the B-29. He began his search for two women at first. In June of 1944, he showed up unannounced at Eglin Air Force Base in Florida. He walked right up to Didi Moorman when she was in the nurse's lounge and asked, "I'm looking for two women of the WASP (Women's Air Support Pilots) to check out the B-29."

She jumped up and saluted. "I have some training in a twin-engine trainer, sir, uh…that's all any of us have except Dora. She's checked out in the A-20." She was referring to Dora Dougherty. He later discovered that she was checked out in twenty-three different military aircraft. These two women had only trained in the B29 for three *days* before they gave a demonstration for the men in the B-29. Usually, the WWII training lasted six months, and these two girls did it in three days! This shamed the men into training in the B-29.

Fortunately, Col. Paul Tibbets, who later became general, flew the B-29, the "Enola Gay," which was named after his mother, and dropped the bomb—code-named "Little Boy"—on Hiroshima on August 6, 1945. This was a uranium bomb. Everyone thought that the devastation and the utter shock of such a bomb would have made Japan surrender. It didn't happen. Then three days later, after hearing nothing from anyone—including the emperor of Japan—and after no sign whatsoever of capitulation on Japan's part, Charles Sweeny, in another B-29 named Bochscar, dropped a plutonium bomb—code-named Fat Man—on Nagasaki on August 9, 1945. Nagasaki happened to be a secondary target. The weather was so cloudy that they couldn't see the primary target, Kokura. Fortunately for Japan, the mountains at Nagasaki helped to hinder the spread of deadly radiation fallout, which could have killed many more people after the fact. There was a third bomb, code-named Thin Man, which, fortunately, was not needed because Japan finally capitulated. On August 15, 1945, Japan surrendered and officially signed the peace treaty with General MacArthur on the battleship *Missouri*, moored in Tokyo Bay on September 2, 1945.

The bombs' code names came from novels written by a writer named Dashiell Hammett, who wrote a series of detective stories that were being broadcast on radio. In reality, this action of dropping these bombs actually saved many more lives than if the United States had gone in with ground troops. Going house to house in direct hand to hand combat would have taken even more years of war. Japan would not have given up any other way. Not only did it shorten the war, but it also saved more than one million American lives, and it saved even more Japanese lives by not having ground troops going in or fire-bombing every city. This brought a quick end to the greatest, costliest world war in the history of the world. Thank God it was over.

Paul's mother never saw the end of the war with Japan. She passed away early that August of double pneumonia. Fortunately, she was able to see the end of the war in Europe. She never again saw her children or grandchildren who were left in Germany.

The United States helped both Germany and Japan rebuild their countries after the war.

Chapter 33

*P*aul and Minnie continued to enjoy listening to the radio. The entire family loved hearing country music, and every Saturday evening, they listened to the Iowa Barn Dance Frolic. Minnie also liked to listen during the day to "The Guiding Light," which was a soap opera—a continuing series featuring stories of the Old Testament, such as the story of the wicked Queen Jezebel. They continued to keep up with the news and always listened to President Roosevelt. In April of 1945, not long after he won his fourth term, President Roosevelt died of a cerebral hemorrhage in Warm Springs, Georgia. He would travel there several times each year to immerse himself in the warm springs that the town was named for. This helped his legs—which were crippled from childhood polio—become somewhat useful to him. He was successful, much of the time, in keeping his infirmity from the public. Unfortunately, however, he had not briefed his vice president, Harry Truman, about the Manhattan Project (the A-bomb project) or much of anything else either. Needless to say, the nation was in mourning for their beloved president, and it was a big load for Truman. It took great courage to carry on with the plan to end the war quickly and contain the number of American casualties.

Truman was now burdened with a huge responsibility, and as a man who believed in God, he was torn with the decision of whether to drop the atomic bomb, but in the end, he was convinced it was the correct thing to do. He weighed every angle and ultimately decided to go ahead with the plan, if things kept going as they were, in order to save the greatest number of lives possible.

The Luzon campaign weighed heavily on his shoulders because of all the young Americans who died there. America was fighting a war on almost every continent and island in the world. His thoughts were that it needed to be over. He was constantly reminded of Pearl Harbor and all the Americans dying all over the world. He was reminded that the United States didn't start this thing, but he was responsible for getting it over with as soon as possible. He was intent on saving as many American lives as humanly possible. This war, for which we didn't ask, was now our responsibility to conclude.

Harry Truman was never afraid of being criticized. He was brutally honest. He even bought his own postage stamps, from his own pocket, for his personal mail. He never took anything for granted, and he had a sign on his desk that said, "The buck stops here." He was a hard worker and was a loving husband to his wife, Bessie, and he adored his daughter, Margaret, who always aspired to be a serious singer. Truman also played the piano and played classical music such as Mozart's *Piano Sonata No. 11*. He loved to play and, as a youngster, never had to be told to practice.

Though it was finally beginning to look as though the war would be coming to an end soon, Florence's war was not finished. Her fight was not yet done, her constant battles not yet over. Paul and Minnie were always there for her, trying to help her survive the constant struggles of coping with a violent and philandering husband while trying to lovingly raise and care for her son as well. Paul and Minnie came over many times and fixed doors, electrical boxes, furniture, and anything else Chuck destroyed when he was home.

By 1944, Florence was beginning to accept the fact that she was not being successful in trying to have another child. In those days, the medical field had few options to try to help her. Her son was now in kindergarten, and she was thinking that she should try to see her parents sometime. She had received a few letters from them, and neither of them seemed in good health. She really missed her family, and she hadn't seen them since she left after her quick marriage. Her heartbreak was that any time she even suggested trying to see her family, Chuck started a fight about how he didn't want to get married in the first place, so "Now reap your bitter reward." In other words,

"You asked for this. Now live with it." He always made it sound like she trapped him into this situation, and now she had to live with it, no matter what he said or did to her. In Florence's mind, it was not her doing. It was his, and sometimes, she thought that if she hadn't gotten pregnant, she could have had a much better life. Sometimes, she thought she should just disappear and not be seen again so that she would not have to endure Chuck's threats, his awful violence, and his degradation all the time.

Florence was getting to feel so done with the whole thing. More than once she discussed with Minnie the possibility of divorce. Paul always was the one who had a positive outlook and said a family needs to stay together. Paul said that he would have a talk with Chuck, and maybe Chuck would actually take her with him on a run to Indiana. Paul, of course, was thinking like an honorable man and didn't see the problem. He didn't think of all the other women Chuck saw while he was away. Paul thought that Etta was the exception, not the rule. Florence began to think it might be possible that Paul could influence him. After all, it had worked a few times before. Minnie or Chuck's parents would be willing to take care of little Butchie in the event Florence could go to visit her folks. Paul and Minnie thought it just might work, especially since it would cost almost nothing. They were always trying to figure out how to save money.

Florence began to think that maybe she would be able to go with Chuck when he went that direction on one of his upcoming runs to Indiana. When she broached the subject with him one evening, he flew into a rage. "I didn't want to bring you here in the first place, and I sure as hell don't want you cramping my style and providing you with something to eat and drink plus a place to sleep while I'm on the road." With that, he started his semi and took off. He, of course, went over to Etta's.

The next morning, Florence went to Paul and Minnie's to see if they could help her figure out a way to get out of this mess. They had a few suggestions, but none seemed feasible at the time. Paul even thought of taking her himself to see her folks in Indiana, but he didn't want to take off work. He knew that he needed to work when the weather cooperated. As Paul was really thinking it over, he finally realized that Chuck was nothing more than a despicable abuser who would never change, and Florence's battles would never be over if she stayed in Parkersburg. Chuck's parents would always bail him out, and things would never be different. He never really had to pay the consequences of his actions. Therefore, it was not to his advantage to change his ways.

A week later, Chuck came in the door from a run, and he had obviously been drinking. He was already out of control and demanded his rights as a husband. Florence did not like the whole idea and was disgusted by his behavior. She tried to get him to eat something or drink some tomato juice or anything to get him to sober up. She thought, at least then, she could cope with the situation. He didn't want to sober up. He became a raging bull. He grabbed her and ripped the clothes off her, beat her, and brutally raped her. "I will have my way with you, you bitch. I can use you till you are dead, and I never have to worry about having to take care of any other stinking brat 'cause you ain't never gonna have another kid I've seen to that, you bitch, your tubes inside are destroyed." All the time, he was laughing at her.

"Ha, ha, I can use you all I want, and I never have to pay for it. No more kids. I had you fixed. It is my right as your husband to do with you what I want, and you have nothing to say about it."

Unfortunately, he was correct in that despicable assumption because women were, and still often are, though maybe to a lesser extent, slaves to their husbands. Finally, after over an hour of abuse, Chuck left. This was as bad as what some of the Russians did to the German women after taking Berlin. Florence was too spent and bleeding to even attempt to get out to safety. She was afraid that he would come back, so she not only locked the doors but also placed furniture in front of them. Then after trying to get herself cleaned up, she collapsed into bed. She wasn't sure that she would live until morning. She wasn't even completely sure she wanted to.

Chapter 34

*I*t was seven o'clock in the morning when Minnie saw Florence—or what seemed to be Florence—come staggering in the door with Butchie in tow.

"I need your help, Minnie. I've gotta leave Chuck. I want to go home. Will you keep Butchie and take him over to Chuck's parents when I leave?"

"Wait a minute, Florence, Paul will be here in a few minutes. He just went to the Johnson's place to check out a job that he is intending to start day after tomorrow if the weather holds. I will help fix you up. You look terrible. What happened?"

Florence told Minnie the whole story. When she told her that Chuck said he had her fixed so she would never have another child, Minnie was appalled. She could hardly believe her ears—especially that a doctor would do such a thing without the patient knowing.

Florence sobbed, "And Chuck laughed about it. He said that it was his right as my husband to do that to me. How can that be?"

Minnie finally spoke up after a long pause and replied, "I have been wondering why it was that you weren't conceiving. I knew something was amiss but couldn't quite put my finger on what it was. My first thought would be, how did Chuck know what needed to be done when he has such limited knowledge of the female body, except for how to use it for his own pleasure? There is something wrong here. All along, I was thinking that maybe there was scar tissue or something keeping you from getting pregnant, and now I find out that the doctor, under orders from your husband, must have cut the other tube as well. My god, Florence, what have they done? It just isn't right!"

164

Minnie burst into tears for her dear friend, and at that moment, she was eternally grateful for her kind and gentle husband who had such a good heart. Finally, lighting up a cigarette, she composed herself. Florence's whole life with Chuck was one battle after another, but this disturbing news was the final clincher. In Minnie's mind, this was Florence's atom bomb. She was not the same anymore, just as the world has not been the same since Hiroshima. This changed her entirely. She would never be the same lovely, optimistic person she was before all this happened. She seemed like the walking dead, and even Florence herself began to think she was just as dead as the many soldiers, sailors, and marines who died at their battle stations. Her battle was done. She really didn't care what happened to her anymore.

Paul walked in the door just then and got a good look at Florence. As she relayed to him what she had told Minnie, Paul couldn't believe what he was hearing. He had had enough of Chuck and all the turmoil he had brought into Florence's life. Enraged, he suddenly burst as if a geyser was shooting through him, announcing that Florence was leaving but that she should never divorce Chuck. That way, he could never marry again and do to another wife what he did to her.

Explaining further, he said, "Vell, Florence, my brudder Bill ran off vit my udder brudder's vife in 1939, and no vun has located dem yet. I tink vee have a good plan. Don't tell anyone vere you are going. Florence," he said. "I vill take you to Vaterloo and see to it dat you get on a train to Indiana. Let's go to your house and get some of your clothes. Vee'll pack dem in boxes here, if necessary, and get you on your vay."

"Paul, I'll take care of Butchie, and we can take him to Chuck's parents when you get back," Minnie offered. "If things work out, maybe she will be able to come back sometime to pick him up and take him to Indiana so that her parents could meet their grandson."

Minnie sobbed into Florence's shoulder as they said their goodbyes.

"Let's go, Florence," Paul called out as he went through the door.

Paul was gone most of the day, but he was back after dark to take Butchie and his things over to Chuck's parents.

Naturally, the Millers were surprised and wondered what was happening. There was speculation that Florence might have found a way to Indiana, or maybe she just somehow disappeared. The story was that Paul went to pick up Butchie so he and Vern could play together for a while, but when he got there, Florence was gone. So he brought Butchie home with him as he had done many times before. That was the story. For all intents and purposes, she had just vanished.

Paul then went over to Marshal Lumley to report Florence missing. He told the marshal that for all anybody knew, Florence had just disappeared. They went over to the house and saw the disarray and some bloodstains on the bed, so it was obvious that there had been a terrible struggle. Then an idea came to them. They could make it seem like Chuck had finally gone too far and ended up killing her. With that threat over his head, maybe Chuck would not try to go looking for her.

Later, after the marshal found Chuck, he questioned him about what had happened. Chuck admitted what he had done to Florence but added, "I didn't kill her, honest." The marshal knew what had really happened because Paul had told him in confidence. But he kept on questioning Chuck and asked him to repeat over and over the happenings of the night.

He told Chuck, "I am not convinced that you had nothing to do with Florence's disappearance because you almost killed her before. Now where did you stash the body?"

"I tell you I didn't kill anybody, I swear," Chuck groaned.

"I tell you, Charles Miller, if I had more evidence, you'd be sleeping in the jail tonight," Harry said, all the while thinking, *I want him to squirm. I want him to feel as uncomfortable as I can possibly make him.* Aloud he said, "If Florence's body is ever found, I will see to it that you hang for it. Now get out of my sight!" shouted Harry as he opened the door to let Chuck out.

Chuck got out of there fast and went over to Etta's for comfort.

Chapter 35

Chuck was now stuck with a house and a son he never wanted. Of course, his parents gladly took Butchie in. They loved their grandchild, even if Chuck didn't.

The house was eventually sold. Chuck never showed his face anywhere in Parkersburg proper after that, and he still worked as a truck driver, but no one saw him around town except possibly Etta. She was questioned about Florence's disappearance by the marshal, just as Chuck had been. But they were both cleared of a murder charge unless a corpse was ever to be found. The marshal did testify that he had found blood at the house and had taken pictures of the scene. He admitted that there was no actual proof that a murder had taken place. The only thing that was certain was that Florence had disappeared. Though Paul had told the marshal the real story, no one ever found out the truth.

It was several years later when Chuck went to the area in Indiana where he and Florence had first met. While there, he found a young couple living in the farmhouse where his in-laws had lived. There was no sign of Florence anywhere, and everyone he talked to said they hadn't seen her. He had told people back home that he was curious but really didn't care if he ever saw her again. He was glad that he was rid of her.

The young couple said that they rented the place about a half a year ago, but they had no idea what happened to the people who had lived there before or where they were. The place had been sold to a Realtor who then rented it out to them. They mentioned that there was a trunk with some things in it that had not been taken when the house was cleaned out. If he was interested, he could take a look to see if there was anything he might want, but he said he was not interested. He didn't want any of "the bitch's stuff."

When Florence had first arrived in Indiana from Iowa, she had gone directly to the farm. To her dismay, she found that her mother had passed away some months back and that Josiah had been trying to keep going and now was very ill. Florence took him to the hospital, where he eventually died of a heart attack. For several days, he was joyful to see his daughter but had regrets about having pushed her into the marriage to Chuck. He asked for her forgiveness. His thoughts, at the time, were that since Chuck would often be coming through their little town because of his job as a trucker, he had assumed that she would be able to come and visit several times during the year. He had regretted not being able to see Florence or her son and had sent mail occasionally, especially after Ruby passed away, but Florence hadn't received any mail. She did send letters, but few were ever received. Chuck made sure letters were not sent or received by Florence if he could help it.

It was said that Josiah and Ruby didn't want to live anymore without their little girl around. They regretted having sent Florence away. They really had thought they were doing the right thing at the time.

After her father's funeral, Florence had a lot to do. She went through the papers at the house and realized that there were many bills that hadn't been paid. She knew that with the latest hospital bills, she would have to sell everything. She filled a couple of suitcases with some of her clothes that were still at the house. Then when all the paperwork was done, she sold the property to a Realtor. She placed some of her favorite pictures and a letter that she had written to her folks announcing the birth of Butchie, which somehow got through to them in the battered old trunk in the attic. There she noticed a dusty old notebook on top of a shelf. She sat down on the trunk and wrote a letter to Paul and Minnie, thanking them for all the help they had given her.

It took several hours and many pages of paper from the worn tablet that was still there to write down all she had been through and her hopes for the future and her dreams to see the country. She put many of her favorite things in the trunk, along with the notebook. She had no envelope, but she wrote Paul and Minnie's address on the last page of the notebook. Then she went downstairs after locking the trapdoor. Later, the house was sold with everything in it, including the land on which it stood.

Florence wound up with enough money to do some sightseeing around the country, living in hotels and motels along the way. This was what she had longed for in her younger years. She actually saw Los Angeles. She was lonely, but she had sufficient money to see the places she had always wanted to see. She did not want to go back to Iowa. She was afraid that Chuck would be able to find her and kill her as he had threatened to do so many times before. Her life was as ruined as the many countries where the war had taken place. As an only child and now with both of her parents gone, she had no support system no matter where she went. Her only true friends—Paul and Minnie, who had helped her out so many times and supported her in so many ways—happened to live in the one place where Chuck could find her. She didn't ever want that to happen. She was glad that to almost everyone in the world, she had disappeared off the face of the earth.

It was a few years later when there was a knock on the door of Paul and Minnie's house late in the evening. There stood Florence with some man! She seemed happy-go-lucky and fun, just like she was when Minnie first met her.

She thanked Paul and Minnie for helping her when she needed it. She had gone by Chuck's parent's house at twilight and actually saw her son but did not approach him. She only wanted to see him. They had parked in the Catholic cemetery to watch him. There was a sparkle in her eye as she talked about her son. Then after dark, they went over to Minnie and Paul's place. Minnie suggested that they park in the barn and opened the door so they could get the car of sight, hoping to keep the secret.

As they talked, Minnie knew that Florence had no intention of filing for divorce because she knew that if there was no divorce, Chuck could never marry again.

After they finished catching up with each other, Florence and her friend stayed overnight, sleeping on blankets on the dining room floor.

At dawn, Minnie had coffee ready and a little breakfast, and they left before the kids got up to get ready for school. They were introduced to the newest little girl in the family, Linda Lou, the only one up at that hour. Of course, she would be up because she was always hungry. She was born that June. Paul did get to see Florence, and she tried to give him the same amount of money that he had given her to get on the train in Waterloo. He, however, would not accept it. He did it for a friend and Minnie's best friend. A few minutes later, however, he had an idea and said, "I vill take it and buy a present for Butchie for Christmas." They all agreed that would be acceptable. The presents would come from his "angel mom." Paul and Minnie, of course, would always welcome her and keep her secret. Apparently, no one ever investigated her disappearance. Women often "disappeared" in those days with little or no notice.

Paul and Minnie were glad to see that Florence seemed happy and satisfied. She seemed to have money, and they were driving a nice car. Her friend seemed to respect her and was always telling her how pretty she was.

This same scenario happened every so often at various times throughout several more years. This way, Minnie knew Florence was okay. Each time, Florence had a different man with her, and Minnie got the feeling that she was selling herself in order to live. She now apparently knew how to use men to get what she wanted. The only thing that mattered to Minnie was that she was a friend, and she was alive. "I guess she needs to use men like she was used by Chuck," she said to herself.

"I sure hope no one ever finds out how we helped Florence and that we have seen her a few times these last few years," Minnie was heard to say to Paul one evening by Wilma. She was always the curious one. But she never revealed the secret to a soul—except to Minnie when she was home from school one day on washday. "I just want you to know, Mom, that the secret is safe with me." It was never mentioned again between the two of them. Florence was to stay "dead" as far as anyone was to know.

Eventually, Minnie had three more girls: Carol Ann, Sandra Lee, and Rita Marie.

As an avid reader of the newspaper, Minnie read every word. It so happened that in the 1960s, Minnie read a story in the paper about a woman named Florence Miller who had been murdered and brutally beaten in a hotel room in Des Moines, Iowa. By then, Minnie hadn't seen or heard a thing from Florence in at least five years. Minnie knew in her heart of hearts that the Florence in the story was her dear friend, Florence.

For most people, Florence was long forgotten but not for Minnie. She cried for her friend for many days. *I wonder*, she thought. *Did Chuck finally find her?*

It could have been a total stranger. It might even have been a "client," but she couldn't help but believe it was really Chuck who had finally tracked her down and murdered her. While Minnie mourned her friend's passing and wondered what might have been, she took comfort in the knowledge that at least Florence's battles were over now.

Nothing was made of her murder. According to the authorities, she was "only a woman of the evening. Not really worth much," except to those who loved her, of course—most especially Minnie, who mourned the loss of her good friend for a long, long time after. The murder was never solved.

In 1970, a strange trunk came to the door of Paul and Minnie's house. The address on the trunk seemed to be a page torn from an old-lined notebook. Accompanying the trunk was a letter from a Realtor in Indiana which stated:

Dear Paul and Minnie Adelmund,

I am the lawyer who was in charge of Florence's parents' estate, and this trunk is all that is left. I found your address inside, along with a letter to you from Florence. I believe that she wanted you to have these things as a way of repaying you for your kindness toward her.

Signed,
Mason B. Gores Sr. Law Firm

When Minnie opened the trunk, she found Florence's lengthy, heartfelt letter to them, along with all the things that she held most dear, some of which Minnie recognized. Anxiously, Minnie began reading:

Dear Paul and Minnie, my dear friends,

I am leaving this trunk in the attic of my parents' home as I leave here. I want you to have these things as a remembrance of me. You did so much to help me…

As Minnie continued reading the letter from her beloved friend, a flood of memories overcame her. She began to weep, haunted by a single thought, "Is this really all that is left of her? Could Florence's life really be so meaningless that it could fit into a beat-up old trunk?"

No one knows if Florence even has a headstone or if she would ever be remembered. Was her murder ever solved? Is the trunk still in existence?

Minnie always wondered if anyone ever saw an unfamiliar car leaving their barn throughout the years. Minnie's wondering is over now. Minnie died in January of 1972. Paul passed away in February of 1982. By 2012, four of Minnie's children had also passed away.

All their private wars are long over. World War II's effects are still felt. Most of the veterans of that terrible war are long gone, but they never will be forgotten. They are still being honored daily.

Florence and her friends are also not forgotten and never will be.

Appendix

Major battles of the war which took place before Americans' declaration of war. (G) indicates that the battle was instigated by Germany. (J) indicates that the battle was instigated by Japan.

1. (G) The Battle of Sedan (France), May 1940.
2. (G) The Battle of the Atlantic, 1940–1943. This was an ongoing battle throughout the war. German U-boats were constantly sinking anything they saw on the Atlantic. Finally, the battle was won due to the new technology of radar to detect U-boats from above, as well as better radio communications, and finally breaking the German code.
3. (G) The Battle of Britain (England), July to October 1940. In this battle, German planes were constantly bombing England.
4. (G) Battle of Crete, May 1941. German soldiers had already taken Greece. The next to conquer was the Island of Crete.
5. (G) Battle of Brody (in Russia's Ukraine), June 1941. This was the beginning of "Barbarossa," the name the Germans called their offensive to capture the Soviet Union.
6. (J) Pearl Harbor was bombed. The United States declared war on December 7–8, 1941, "a day that will live in infamy."
7. (G) Battle of Moscow (Russia), October 1941 to January 1942. German momentum was broken—one million people killed, including civilians. America was at war.

8. (J) The Battle of the Coral Sea in the South Pacific near the Solomon Islands and New Guinea, May 1942. After this battle, the Japanese were forced to call off their pending invasion plans of the area.

9. (G) The Second Battle of Kharkov (Russia), May 1942.

10. (J) The Battle of Midway, June 1942. This was a victory for the allies, near the island of Midway in the Pacific Ocean, and was a morale boost to the United States. This was a real miracle for the United States because it was a small task force that somehow beat a superior Japanese fleet.

11. (G) The Battle of Stalingrad, August 1942 to February 1943. There were two million casualties (both sides).

12. (J) The *Juneau* is sunk by the Japanese on November 13, 1942, killing the Sullivan brothers, Minnie's childhood friends. There was no significant battle. It was a random act. The Japanese saw an American ship and simply sank her.

13. (G) The Battle of Kursk, July to August 1943. This was the final German offensive in Russia.

14. (G) The Battle of Anzio (Italy), January to June 1944. The battles in Italy, especially in the mountainous areas, were brutal. This is a battle that lasted half a year.

15. (G) The Battle of Monte Cassino, January to May 1944. This is another Italian campaign.

16. (J) The Battle of the Philippine Sea, June 1944. Four thousand were killed, and one thousand nine hundred were wounded.

17. (J) The Battle of the Leyte Gulf, October 23–26, 1944, near the Philippine Islands—probably the largest naval battle in history. This is the first time an American experienced a kamikaze pilot sacrificing himself. He crashed on purpose on the deck of the USS carrier *St. Loa*.

18. (G) The Battle of the Bulge, December 16, 1944, to January 18, 1945. This was the last German offensive, located in Northern France. The Eighth Army had its headquarters in Bastogne, Belgium. At a time when the Germans thought

the Americans might consider surrender, a runner was sent to ask the Americans to surrender. He was sent back with a note. The only thing the Americans wrote on the paper was "nuts," possible meaning, "you Germans must be nuts." Whatever it meant, with the arrival of General George S. Patton, they broke out and won the battle. Whatever people think of him, Patton was a great man. Sometimes, you have to get radical to get the job done any way you can. He got the job done. He will always be a hero to the American people no matter how he is demonized by some who were not even alive when WWII happened. May he rest in peace. General Patton was the only American General of whom the Germans were afraid. German General Rommel considered him a worthy adversary.

19. (J) The Battle of Iwo Jima, February 19 to March 26, 1945. The American flag was raised on Mount Suribachi, February 23, 1945, and the picture was in the American newspapers; therefore, many Americans thought the battle was over, and the war was certain to be over also. This came at a time when people were tired of the killing and the maiming of young Americans. They just wanted it to be over, and the sooner, the better. Americans had already lost so much. That picture ultimately became an iconic reminder of the Battle of Iwo Jima.

There were still Japanese in the tunnels long after the major battle was over. They still were sought after because they caused trouble for the Americans stationed there throughout the length of the war. Iwo Jima became an air base close enough to Japan to use the B29s. This is an island of approximately 8 square miles. Six thousand eight hundred Americans were killed there. That amounts to 850 deaths per square mile. The island was taken from the Japanese, but it took over a month of intense fighting. It had been shelled by the US Navy prior to the landing. The shelling didn't do much good, it seems, because the landing, that first day, took the lives of two thousand marines.

20. (G) The Battle of Berlin, April to May 1945. On the thir-
tieth of April 1945, Adolph Hitler killed himself. Many
of his followers did likewise. General Patton was told that
he could not go into Berlin. Some say that he would have
been a gentleman and treated the Germans well, as it was;
however and whatever Eisenhower's motivations were, no
one knows, but he allowed the Russians to go in first. What
happened was horrific. What they did to the German
women was too awful to describe. Many were hauled off to
slave labor in Siberia. Some people were never heard from
again. This would never have happened under Patton.
Three quarters of a million people tried to defend Berlin
with no leadership against the Russians who were out to get
revenge any way they could.

21. (J) The Battle of Luzon, January to August 1945. This is
the largest of the Philippine Islands. This was the blood-
iest action of the war for American lives. Ten thousand
Americans lost their lives.

CPSIA information can be obtained
at www.ICGtesting.com
Printed in the USA
LVHW092204040421
683422LV00024B/343